"FEED AT RAFFLES when visiting SINGAPORE" — Rudyard Kipling

Published by Raffles Hotel (1886) Pte Ltd
A Raffles International Hotel

Project Director: Gretchen Liu
Chefs: Executive Chef Jean Paul Naquin and his culinary team
Editor: Melisa Teo
Designers: Tan Seok Lui and Tan Tat Ghee

Editorial: Angus Cameron and Harry Tan
Design Concept: Duet Design Pte Ltd

Produced by Editions Didier Millet Pte Ltd
121 Telok Ayer Street, Singapore 068590
Tel: (65) 6324 9260 Fax: (65) 6324 9261
Email: edm@edmbooks.com.sg

Printed in Singapore

The following Heritage Search donations have been used as illustrations in this book:
– Photograph of Ngiam Tong Boon, page 27, donated by Arthur Ngiam, Singapore
– 1929 Grill Room menu card, page 40, donated by Mr. B.H. White, Essex, England
– Photograph of 1937 Australian Day dinner at Raffles Hotel, page 25, donated by Mrs. G. Kennett, New South Wales, Australia

First published 1994
Reprinted 1995, 2000
Second edition 2003

Page 4-5: A 1915 portrait of Raffles Hotel.
Page 6: Raffles Hotel at its re-debut in 1991.

ISBN: 981-4068-58-6

The
RAFFLES HOTEL
COOKBOOK

Recipes by the Raffles Hotel Chefs

Photography by Luca Invernizzi Tettoni and Gerald Gay

Introduction by Gretchen Liu

Raffles Editions

Contents

FEED AT RAFFLES

This cookbook opens the doors of Raffles Hotel's restaurants and kitchens, taking a nostalgic look at a tradition of hospitality that began over a century ago and sharing recipes for some of the most popular dishes served today. Since the hotel reopened in 1991, after a two-and-a-half year restoration process, Raffles' culinary team has consistently won rave reviews.

Each of the hotel's restaurants serves a unique cuisine — from the continental classics of Raffles Grill, to the Anglo-Indian curries of the Tiffin Room; from the Singaporean hawker dishes of the Empire Cafe, to the exotic take on the traditional fare of the Long Bar Steakhouse; from the trans-ethnic flavours of Doc Cheng's, to the Cantonese favourites of the Empress Room; from the seafood and tapas enjoyed *al fresco* in Raffles Courtyard, to the Seah Street Deli with its New York-style sandwiches and the fresh daily treats of Ah Teng's Bakery.

There are also four unique bars: the beautifully restored Bar and Billiard Room, the Writer's Bar, the outdoor Pool Bar, and the historic Long Bar, where visitors continue to undergo one of the true rites of passage of world travel — savouring the delights of a Singapore Sling. Such diversity, strange though it may seem to those unfamiliar with the island of Singapore, is quintessentially Singaporean. And quintessentially Raffles.

~

Situated at the southern tip of the Malay Peninsula, the island of Singapore has always been at the crossroads of Asia. In ancient times Chinese junks and the ships of Indian and Arab traders passed by laden with precious cargoes. By the 5th century A.D. the island was known as Temasek and formed part of the powerful Srivijaya empire of Sumatra; by the 13th century the island had been renamed "Singa Pura", Sanskrit for "City of the Lion", and had become an important outpost of the Javanese Majapahit empire, only to be destroyed during a Javanese-Siamese power struggle in the 15th century.

The Tiffin Room (left), an elegant recreation of the original Main Dining Room, serves breakfast, lunch, high tea and dinner.

For several centuries Singapura slumbered on, its past kept alive in legends. Malay pirates occupied its shores, living between jungle and sea, and watching the arrival of the Portuguese and Dutch traders who now began their scramble for the lucrative spice trade of the Indonesian Archipelago.

Modern Singapore was founded by a brash but scholarly officer of the British East India Company who knew and loved these legends and understood the language and customs of the Malayan world. He is also the hotel's namesake. In 1819 Sir Thomas Stamford Raffles stepped ashore and signed a treaty with the Temenggong, the local Malay ruler, which allowed him to establish a trading base there. The entire island was ceded to the East India Company in 1824, by which time Singapore's future looked exceedingly bright. Raffles' vision of "a great commercial empire" and his free-trade policy began to attract ambitious immigrants from Penang and Malacca, Java and Sumatra, southern China and India, and virtually all points in between.

A new town was quickly carved out of jungle and mangrove swamp, its buildings clustered along the seafront and Singapore River where godowns soon filled with all the treasures of the East. To ensure orderly urban growth, Raffles bequeathed Singapore a town plan that set aside land for government use (today's Civic District), a public green (the Padang), a commercial centre (Raffles Place) and a separate enclave for each of the distinct ethnic groups.

By 1887 — the year in which a young Armenian hotelkeeper, Tigran Sarkies, opened a new hotel and

named it after Sir Stamford — Singapore had become a permanent, major entrepôt on the East-West trade route. Officially declared a Crown Colony in 1867, the island was home to the British Governor of the Straits Settlements of Singapore, Malacca and Penang. The opening of the Suez Canal in 1869 and the advent of steamships speeded up the transportation of goods and travellers, and the seafront was soon jammed with these large coal-fed vessels alongside Chinese junks and Malay prahus.

In the early years of this century, when the mystique of the British Empire was at its height and Raffles Hotel was earning its reputation as "the finest Caravanserai east of Suez", Singapore was becoming one of the world's busiest ports and a focus of the trading wealth of the Malay Peninsula. Above all, it was the most cosmopolitan city in Asia. Its streets thronged with a continuous stream of colourful immigrants, sojourners and globetrotters.

The ethnic — and culinary — balance that today makes Singapore so remarkable was even then in place: seventy-five percent Chinese, fifteen percent Malay, seven percent Indian and three percent "others", including Eurasians. Each group brought with it and retained its own customs, social structure, religious practices, temples, festivals, superstitions and, of course, food. The communal solidarity was reinforced as newcomers gravitated to their own ethnic areas.

The ranks of the small, original Malay community soon swelled with arrivals of Peninsular Malays, Sumatrans, Javanese, Buginese and Boyanese.

Bound together by a common faith, Islam, by the Malay language and by centuries of contact, the gentle, seafaring Malays left the bulk of trade and commerce to the soon dominant Chinese. The Malays had dealt with Arab and Indian traders for generations, and the typical Malay seasonings, including pepper, cardamom, ginger, and dishes such as *nasi briyani* (rice cooked with aromatic spices and meat), or *satay*, a spicy kebab, reveal the centuries of foreign influence.

Singapore's early Chinese population was mostly male and almost exclusively from southern China, although from different provinces and speaking different dialects. The Hokkiens from southern Fujian and the city of Amoy were the largest group. Next came the Teochews from east Guangdong and the Cantonese from southern Guangdong. There were smaller groups of Hainanese, or Hailams, from the southern island of Hainan (these were well represented in Raffles' kitchens and bars and included the creator of the Singapore Sling, Ngiam Tong Boon), as well as Hakkas, Hokchius and Hokchias. Today you can, quite literally, eat your way through China in Singapore, from the sophisticated and mild cooking of northern China to the seafood dishes and heavier stews of the Teochews and Hokkiens, from Hainanese chicken rice to the chilli-garlic flavoured dishes of Szechuan or, as in Raffles' Empress Room, the much admired cooking of the Cantonese.

Long before the large-scale immigration of Chinese in the 19th century, however, numerous Chinese traders lived in Malacca, where they married Malay women. This gave rise to a unique ethnic community known as the Straits Chinese, or Peranakans. The men, called Babas, eventually stopped taking Malay brides and married Straits Chinese women, or Nonya, although Nonyas often wed recent arrivals from China approved by their parents. The Straits Chinese were an influential group in colonial Singapore. They were pro-British and English speaking, in addition to their own version of Malay, and their cooking evolved into a complex Chinese-Malay blend, that is considered by many to be the truly Singaporean cuisine. It is much loved even today.

Singapore's Indian population has always been diverse: soldiers and convicts brought out under the aegis of the East India Company; Chettier moneylenders; Gujerati, Sikh, Sindhi and Indian Muslim textile and jewellery merchants;

Tamil and Malayali labourers who dominated the docks and railways; and a handful of English-educated professionals from the subcontinent and Sri Lanka (Ceylon). Large groups of Tamils from the southern Indian state of Madras also arrived as indentured labourers to tap rubber in Malaya. Their dominant numbers ensured a place for Tamil among Singapore's four national languages, alongside Malay, Mandarin and English. Thus Singapore's Indian food embraces both the hot spicy dishes of the south and the more mild aromatic dishes of the north. For a taste of India, Singaporeans often head to the restaurants in Little India, the historic district with its labyrinth of lanes off Serangoon Road.

The colony's European population was never very large, yet as the ruling class in colonial Singapore it was

Raffles Hotel may have opened modestly in 1887 (left) but from the outset every effort was made by Sarkies Brothers, Hotel Proprietors, to tempt travellers' tastebuds. The watercolour of the hotel (above) is dated 1899.

disproportionately powerful. And yes they, too, brought their culinary habits, initially maintaining a meat and potatoes diet that only gradually began to include Asian flavours. The Eurasians were a mixed community embracing people of Portuguese and Dutch extraction from Malacca as well as Anglo-Indians and Anglo-Chinese. Eurasian food is, not surprisingly, a varied blend of Eastern and Western flavours, dishes and cooking techniques rarely found today outside the homes of Singapore's old Eurasian families.

The disparity of these ethnic groups did not, however, preclude their enjoyment of each other's food. Indian curries, Malay satay and Chinese noodles knew no cultural barriers so long as the ingredients did not offend religious practices. (Muslims do not eat pork, Chinese Buddhists and Indian Hindus, beef.) Somewhere along the way, Singaporeans' unrivalled passion for all foods was born.

The long association of the groups also led to the alteration of traditional habits: life alongside the chilli-loving Malays and Indians resulted in the Chinese appreciating a touch of heat in their food. These days, Singaporeans of all races will sit down to a Western breakfast of buttered toast or, more recently, croissants and Danish pastries.

Among the early influential figures in this crossing of food barriers were the humble street hawkers. These itinerant food sellers roamed the streets with their portable restaurants — a pole slung over the shoulder, cooking apparatus at one end and a table on the other — offering cooked fare at low cost. The quality of the victuals was, of course, entirely up to the vendor, but a famous hawker could become a legend.

The hawker cooking style, which is largely dependent on quick cooking and includes a multitude of soups, fried noodles and seafood dishes, eventually became synonymous with Singaporean food. A visitor to Singapore summed it up in 1933: "The French proletariat feed on *pâté de fois gras* in a restaurant on the *pavé*, the English in a stuffy Lyons or A.B.C. on a bun or beef steak, the American in a dive with the atmosphere of a Smoke House on sandwiches, and the Straits-born Chinese in God's fresh air on delectable well-cooked foods."

Although hawkers were moved off the streets several decades ago and resettled into permanent hawker centres, their food remains a staple and much loved component of the Singaporean diet. Indeed, in the 1970s many typically hawker dishes began appearing on the menus of the Orchard Road five-star hotel coffee shops. They can also be enjoyed in Raffles Hotel's Empire Cafe.

~

This singular variety of cuisines is, however, but one component of Singapore's culinary history. Equally important has been the bounty and freshness of the ingredients available. Singapore has long benefitted from a rich supply of edibles of all kinds and even today it is in the "wet" market that Malay, Indian, Chinese, Eurasian, Peranakan and European alike make their selection of fresh fish, fowls, vegetables and fruits.

By 1900, the town area boasted five famed markets. The elaborate cast-iron Telok Ayer Market stood along the

Portraits of hawkers and household help (above) were among the photographs purchased as souvenirs by 19th century travellers. The postcard from the "East And West" (right) series sums up kitchen differences a century ago.

waterfront, near the edge of Chinatown (restored, it is now a festival marketplace). The Clyde Terrace Market bordered Kampong Glam between Beach Road and the sea. Ellenborough Market catered to inhabitants along the Singapore River from its bankside position near New Bridge Road. Rochor Market, in the district of that name, and Orchard or Tanglin Market along Orchard Road served their surrounding areas. The bounty left a vivid impression on many a visitor over the years. One of the best descriptions, however, was published in 1887, the year Raffles Hotel opened its doors, in *A Trip Around the World* by W.S. Caine:

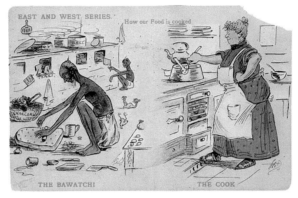

"Singapore, like every other Eastern town, is well off in this respect and the supply of food of all sorts is as usual in the hands of the industrious Chinese, who catch the fish, grow the vegetables and fruit, raise the ducks and poultry and import the beef and mutton ... All round Singapore are small farms in which pigs are reared for the market, and ducks are hatched by artificial incubation. One of these hatching establishments rears from 25,000 to 30,000 ducks every month ... After ducks come fish, which are caught in giant quantities in the bays and straits of the archipelago of islands ... and which are brought to market fresh, or rather alive, twice a day, at dawn and at two in the afternoon. Cuttle fish are in great demand; crabs shaped like long-tailed fans, whose tails are full of green eggs about the size of a pea, are also a great delicacy. Prawns, six inches long, are prized for curry, and the variety of fish of all sizes ranges from a 12-foot shark to the tiniest transparent whitebait. One whole side of the market is given up to dried and salt fish, which made one thirsty even to look at it. Another avenue is devoted to 'chow chow' or cooked food of all sorts, where groups of Chinese and Malays were squatted about enjoying fearsome looking dainties of various kinds and flavours. The meat supply comes from Siam and India, and the fowls mainly from Cochin China and the Malay Peninsula ... the far famed mangosteen ... large pineapples, great clusters of golden bananas and mangoes, green-skinned oranges, persimmons from China, Iychees, custard apples, coconuts and other tropical fruits were displayed in tempting profusion."

There were, in addition, numerous Chinese and Indian provisioners who stocked all manner of dry goods, and emporiums such as Katz Brothers, Robinson's and John Little, who in the 19th century supplied imported tinned foods, preserves, wines and beers from Europe. The Singapore Cold Storage Company's first consignment of frozen meat, fresh butter and fruit arrived from Australia in 1905. By the 1930s Singapore was enjoying fresh meat and rhubarb from Australia, fresh butter from New Zealand, sweet turnips from Sumatra, potatoes from Palestine, tomatoes from Java, oranges from China, and cabbages, lettuce and salads from the Malayan hill station of Cameron Highlands.

To diversity and bounty a third and equally important component of Singapore's culinary heritage must be added:

hospitality. "The people of Singapore are very hospitable, and if you are at all agreeable and appreciative you cannot other than have a good time," recorded a visitor once. Here the sharing of meals has always been basic to human relationships. Food is about friendship and fellowship. As Horace Bleackly, another visitor, observed in the 1920s: "The hospitality of the people of Singapore is embarrassing in its profusion. Nothing could be more kind than my welcome from every one to whom I had an introduction. It was not long before I discovered why the residents looked so healthy and were so healthy ... It is because of the excellence of the food."

Today Singapore is, of course, a very different place from the port city seen by the early travellers quoted here. Independent since 1959 and a full-fledged nation since 1965, it has dramatically reshaped its skyline and coastline, strengthened its economy, transformed its infrastructure, and produced a new breed of Singaporeans from its disparate racial groups.

Happily, the culinary essentials remain. Singapore endures as an exciting gourmet's crossroads, its markets and supermarkets filled with the bounty of the earth and seas, while hundreds of restaurants turn out, quite literally, any dish in the world. Singaporean hospitality continues to leave a lasting impression on visitors from abroad. Raffles Hotel, having made its welcome re-debut, once again hosts travellers with old-fashioned dignity, efficiency and civility. But, above all, Singaporeans remain passionately dedicated to their food.

~

Western travellers' enjoyment of Singapore's food, however, developed gradually. Victorian globetrotters generally viewed food as an aspect of travel to be endured, not enjoyed. Asian food was approached with caution or even disdain. In some circles it was considered unsuitable for the European palate, an outlook that may have reinforced the visitor's sense of security and superiority in a strange place. Most 19th-century visitors dined in the safety of the town's few tiffin rooms and the dining rooms of the European-run hotels — the Hotel de L'Europe, Adelphi Hotel and Hotel de la Paix were all well established before Raffles — which offered typical heavy Victorian fare augmented by Anglo-Indian curries. There was no attempt at style. Guests usually congregated around common tables and were served by Chinese "boys" who handed the dishes around. Food not consumed at one meal was often reheated and dished up at the next.

Among the many Victorian travel writers who stopped in at Singapore, surprisingly few recorded their dining experiences. One of the earliest references appears in the 1840 journal of Edward H. Cree, a surgeon who dined in the London Hotel on "pork chops, curried fowl, roast duck, ham, cheese and potatoes" washed down with "good beer, madeira and claret." Another came from F.W. Burbridge, a botanist and author of *The Gardens of the Sun*, who visited the island in the 1880s. Of the food in his unnamed

In 1892 Tigran Sarkies opened Raffles Tiffin Rooms (right). It remained a popular rendezvous until its closure circa 1910. The pineapple postcard (above) is from the 1890s.

hotel he remarked: "As a rule, everything is well cooked, and there is variety enough for everybody." Breakfast, for example, consisted of "Beef-steaks and mutton chops, one or two well-made curries and rice, eggs and bacon, cold ham, boiled eggs, salads, vegetables and plenty of fresh fruit, washed down with bottled Bass, claret or Norwegian beer."

The dinner party of a well-to-do resident English merchant was an entirely different, and much more elaborate, affair. Mr Burbridge found the host's dinner table laid in European style, "the silver, glass and flower arrangements irreproachable". The dinner itself consisted of "oxtail and 'birds' nest, the latter extremely good but perhaps rather too sweet for European liking; fish of several kinds, beef and mutton cooked in various ways, also pork cutlets excellently cooked ... pastry, cheese, and such fruits for dessert as no money could procure from Covent Garden. Fat juicy mangoes, delicate mangosteen, rambutan, bananas ... ."

Among the memorable dinner parties recorded for posterity were those hosted by two of the most prominent members of the settlement's Asian community, the wealthy Chinese merchant Whampoa Hoo Ah Kay and the Sultan of Johore. Both were exceedingly fond of inviting important visitors and entertained in a style that drew superlatives from guests. Whampoa dined in his famed residence along Serangoon Road, with its elaborate Chinese gardens and stock of superb French Champagne; the Sultan of Johore in his Palace across the Johore Straits where, recalled a guest in the mid-1870s, "the dinner was cooked and served in European style; the table decorated with gold and silver epergnes full of flowers, on velvet stands, and with heaps of small cut flower glasses full of jasmine."

Over time and with increased contact, food barriers gradually disappeared. The shift from endurance test to gourmet paradise is trackable through various travel compendiums and travellers' tales published over the last century.

Some of the earliest advice to travellers is found in the pioneering 1874 edition of Bradshaw's *Through Routes, Overland Guide and Handbook to India, Egypt, Turkey, China, Australia and New Zealand,* which may have been the first guidebook to include Singapore as a traveller's destination. On the subject of food Mr Bradshaw's brevity is remarkable, in contrast to the detailed instructions on the amount and type of clothing to pack or climatic conditions to be encountered. Bradshaw's singular advice was on the "absolute necessity" of maintaining regular mealtimes — 6 am a cup of coffee, 9 am breakfast, 1 pm tiffin (luncheon) and 7 pm dinner. Under the heading "System of Diet" he noted that the East "is as safe as home provided fair precautions are taken ... Eat nourishing food but all kinds of stimulants such as pale ale, brandy, diluted with water, port wine, champagne, etc should be taken in moderate quantities."

Wealthy 19th-century merchant Whampoa Hoo Ah Kay (above) frequently entertained travellers in his famous garden, serving them French champagne. The rickshaw illustration (right) is from a 1930s Dutch travel publication.

The sin of overindulgence was at the core of the advice meted out in *Tropical Trials: A Handbook for Women in the Tropics*, published in 1883: "In the tropics the question is one of paramount importance. Not only the nature of the food, but the quantity thereof ought to be carefully considered, for, while in temperate climates, any injudicious indulgence in the pleasures of the table is only attended with temporary indisposition, a like course in a hot climate would be followed by a train of disasters, often of a gravest description, and which sometimes result in permanent injury to the health."

By the time the 1905 *Souvenir of Singapore Visitor's Guide* made its appearance, the aromatic flavours of India, braised, fried and steamed delicacies of China, and the spicy seasonings of the Malay world were being appreciated. Edwin Brown, writing in the early 1930s about his early years in Singapore circa 1900 recalled: "Very good curry used to be obtained from the hawkers in the five-foot way and we used to toss to see who should provide the staff with a plate each." The 1905 *Guide* counsels that a "new-comer should be careful of the food he takes, and he will find he has a lot to learn in this direction. He has to learn what will agree and what will not with him, and so on. But he can be well guided by the menus of the local hotels, and with a little care and common sense should not suffer much on account of the climate."

With each passing decade the pace of discovery of Singapore's culinary wonders quickened. "It takes at least 24 hours to find one's bearings here. Everything is so different ... All sorts of things are surprising. The food is surprising," wrote Alfred Viscount Northcliffe in the early 1920s.

Guidebooks were also becoming more elaborate and detailed in their discussions of food to be enjoyed — or approached with apprehension. "Uncooked vegetables are the most to be shunned," admonished Cuthbert Woodville Harrison in *An Illustrated Guide to the Federated Malay States* in 1923. "That delight in cool climates — the salad, in all its forms — is dangerous in the East for you cannot be certain whether the water which washed it was pure or the methods of the grower entirely beyond sanitary suspicion."

The author continued: "Another frequent cause of sudden offendings is the Malay curry eaten without understanding. This dish, for those who like spiced meats, is a joy, but like other violent delights it is apt to have violent ends, and it should be eaten with strict moderation. Particularly should one shun the little dried prawns which appear so innocently amongst the *sambals* or little side dishes which accompany the main dish of curried fowl. They have been known to set up a poisoning which may be ptomaine or may be merely a form of shell-fish poisoning, but whatever it be it is exceedingly painful, often dangerous, and has been before now fatal. Surfeits of tropical fruit may be responsible for much discomfort. Milk unboiled is, for a certainty, mixed with water, and the water, for a probability, mixed with typhoid ... The commonest drink is whiskey and soda taken very mild. Most people avoid pork ... The large fresh pink prawn, with its leafy bed of salad and its mayonnaise sauce, is frequently best admired rather than consumed ... Tinned meats are all very well, but fresh are better where obtainable ... It is not intended absolutely to condemn all these foods, but to warn the traveller that unless he is careful he may find that they may prove refractory to his powers of assimilation."

In the 1920s, when Singapore first experienced tourism on a significant scale, with the arrival of luxury passenger ships, dining in Chinatown's crowded and noisy restaurants became positively *de rigueur.* Horace Bleackly, writing in 1928, called Chinese restaurants one of the "important sideshows of Singapore ... where every traveller who is interested in the manners and customs of the East ought to take luncheon." But atmosphere wasn't the only attraction. As another traveller added enthusiastically: "To enumerate the exotic dishes of which we were fortunate to partake would sound more like a poem than a menu."

Even street hawkers were no longer taboo. "One of the joys of the East is the food. Eastern dishes and Eastern methods have very little in common with the accustomed gastronomic conventions of the West. They strike an unaccustomed note on the Western palate, a note which is more than welcome," recorded John MacCallum Scott in *Eastern Journey* in 1939. Mr MacCullum proposed sleuthing street hawkers and in particular the partaking of satay, the small skewered sticks of meat cooked in the open air and eaten with a peanut sauce: "The sati (*sic*) man occupies about the same position of esteem as the ice-cream man in England on a hot summer afternoon. When he sets up his stall at the edge of the pavement, and sets about preparing his *chef d'oeuvre*, crowds begin to flock around him. Even Europeans come to him, and squat down on the edge of the pavement to partake of the delicacy."

One highly visible satay fan was Malcolm MacDonald, the British Commissioner General in the early 1950s. Han Suyin, writing in the American travel magazine *Holiday* recorded that one of the sights of Singapore was to see him "eating at a hawker's stall, on the five-foot way, unperturbed by the grinning, friendly jostling crowds around him. His attitude is the despair of the police who think he should have a whining escort of siren-fitted motorcycles, and a scandal to the old type of colonial Englishman, whose mental isolationism cuts him off from the thought and feeling of Asian Singapore."

By the 1960s Singapore's reputation as a "gourmet paradise" was not only firmly established but becoming increasingly important as the newly independent republic began promoting tourism on an unprecedented scale. Advised one of the many guidebooks of the decade: "Singapore food is as varied and exotic as the goods in its shops. English and Continental cuisine, including menus from famous French, Italian, Swiss and Russian chefs can be ordered in most high class dining places. But the traveller from the West is obviously out to sample the gastronomic specialities of the East." Another guidebook devoted no fewer than 16 pages to wining and dining, advising: "Because of its cosmopolitan population, Singapore has one of the most varied collections of night clubs, restaurants, cafes and to give them their local name, 'coffee shops', in the world. Here you can spend a small fortune on the most exotic food or you can spend very little

*By 1915 Raffles' (above)
reputation was firmly established.
The Sarkies brothers (right)
also founded the Eastern and
Oriental Hotel in Penang and the
Strand Hotel in Rangoon.*

on simple but still fascinating fare." And when the *New York Times* food critic Craig Claiborne visited in 1974 he lamented: "It would require months to pretend any comprehensive coverage of all (or even most) of Singapore's restaurants. They exist at every turn and on every level."

So it is today.

~

It is tempting to think that Tigran Sarkies was guided by the principle that the ultimate test of a hotel is its cuisine. Certainly dining at Raffles Hotel appears from the start to have been different. Although it opened modestly as a 10-room hostelry, the management seems to have paid more attention to food than was normal in Singapore hotels at the time, and the very first advertisement announced: "Sarkies Brothers beg to intimate that they are prepared to undertake Catering for Breakfasts, Tiffins, Dinners and Suppers for Public Balls and Entertainments. Cuisine served at separate tables."

The first accolade bestowed on Raffles' food was penned by Rudyard Kipling in 1889. The now famous quote goes: "Providence conducted me along a beach, in full view of five miles of shipping — five solid miles of masts and funnels — to a place called Raffles Hotel, where the food is as excellent as the rooms are bad. Let the traveller take note. Feed at Raffles and sleep at the Hotel de L'Europe." Kipling so enjoyed his meal at Raffles that, after a visit to the Botanic Gardens, he "crept back" in order to "eat six different chutneys with one curry".

Kipling's words appeared in a column supplied to a newspaper in India as he travelled the globe. After becoming famous, the columns were collected and published in *From Sea to Sea*. Raffles celebrated with a special "Feed at Raffles" dinner on 1st April 1905. In the spirit of April Fool's Day, Kipling's words were paraphrased: "The truth must be told. Providence led me to a place called Raffles Hotel where the food is as excellent as the rooms are good. Let the traveller take note: Feed at Raffles and sleep at Raffles." It was no empty boast. By then, Raffles was very different from the hostelry seen by Kipling.

During its first decade Raffles Hotel expanded under the capable guidance of Tigran Sarkies, one of the four brothers who ran the firm of Sarkies Brothers, Hotel Proprietors. His two younger brothers were busy elsewhere: Aviet opened the Strand Hotel in Rangoon in the 1890s, while Arshak took over the management of the family's first establishment, the Eastern and Oriental in Penang, from eldest brother Martin who retired to the family home in Persia.

Tigran Sarkies' particular interest in culinary matters is evidenced by his opening of Raffles Tiffin Rooms in 1892 (the same year Maxim's opened in Paris). Located in busy Commercial Square — today's Raffles Place — he advertised that hotel residents now had the advantage of being able to "tiffin in town" at his "First Class Tiffin Room". An early advertisement promises: "Cuisine of Highest Character is served at separate tables."

While there is no way of knowing whether Tigran Sarkies introduced caviar to Singapore, the menus for both the hotel and Tiffin Rooms' 1893 New Year's Day celebration commenced with

the delicacy. The advertisement for the event was unusual because it listed the entire lavish menu: Caviar on Toast followed by two soups, Mock Turtle and Bouillon, then Fish Pie, Beefsteak with Oyster Sauce, Roast Spatch Cock with Bread Sauce, Game Pot, Roast Venison with Current Jelly, Roast Turkey stuffed with Truffles and Sausages and Roast Veal; Iced Asparagus, Potatoes, Green Peas, Spinach and Cabbage Salad. And, in addition, two curries, chicken and dry duck. For sweets, Orange Jelly, Rhubarb Tart and Cocoa Ice Cream.

In 1897 Raffles Tiffin Rooms moved into larger quarters, still in Commercial Square, and the ground floor was transformed into a fashionable international *bodega*, or wine cellar: "The arches, covered with cork, give this apartment that vault-like appearance that every orthodox *bodega* presents," reported the press. "Polished casks, of course, form the tables, and there is also a reading table, laden with up-to-date periodical literature. The first floor will be the Raffles Tiffin Rooms and here fully two hundred people will be able to lunch in comfort. The place is well lighted and punkas are there to ensure coolness. The domestic offces are conveniently placed, so that meals may be quickly and properly served."

A circa 1925 view of the Main Dining Room (above) and a hotel postcard from 1904 (right).

Impressive as the changes were, they paled in comparison to those at the hotel where, in 1899, Raffles' architectural centrepiece, the handsome main building, opened. Virtually the entire verandah-enclosed ground floor was occupied by an enormous dining room capable of seating 500 people. It was designed to impress. And it did. Singapore had never seen anything like it before. "Admittedly the most spacious and beautiful public banquet hall in Asia," enthused *The Straits Times*. Two early descriptions convey its grandeur and the impression it made on the public.

The first, from an 1897 newspaper report, will strike a familiar chord with those who have recently stood in what is now the lobby:

"The dining hall is approached from the centre of the front verandah and is T-shaped in plan. It is a very large and beautifully decorated room, 98 feet wide and 67 feet long, and the wings are 36 feet wide. The centre portion of the hall is carried up by the full height of the building, with galleries running round on both of the upper floors, and having a richly ornamented skylight and ventilator on top. The room is divided up by columns and arches, and the walls are richly moulded and decorated. The doors of the dining hall, opening on to the side verandas, are very large and massive and of pleasing design, and ample means of lighting and ventilation are provided ... To the right and left of the private staircase are two private dining rooms, a small one on the left and a large one on the right."

The second comes from the 1913 edition of a popular compendium entitled *Seaports of the Far East*:

"The chief glory of the hotel is its magnificent dining hall, overlooked by balconies on the upper floors. Its handsome pillars, its white Carrara marble floor, and the dainty and artistic arrangement of its numerous tables form an ensemble unsurpassed outside Europe and America; and at night, when dinner is in progress, to the accompaniment of the excellent orchestra, the gay and festive scene is one to be remembered. The culinary departments are replete with the latest appliances, and are in charge of expert European chefs; while the choice vintages and blends in the wine cellars will gladden the most fastidious connoisseurs."

The proximity of the sea, then lapping at the shore on the other side of Beach Road, further endeared the room to discerning travellers. "There is a room in Singapore the town where you can sit and watch the ships of the world go by," wrote a visitor circa 1910. "You can sit at your table and see all this if you face the right way, for the sea swims off blue through all the wide doors and openings. The room that you sit in is huge and white and cool ... There are big pillars and a high sort of dome that ends in a skylight and to most of the pillars are fastened whirring electric fans. And so you sit and are comforted by the cool whirring above you."

To produce the cuisine appropriate to such a grand setting, Tigran Sarkies hired two experienced French chefs in 1900. Their arrival was advertised and their credentials given as having been "employed in the leading hotels and restaurants of France and America — Chez Brébant and Grand Hôtel in Paris and Brunswick Hotel in New York and the Maryland

FRONT VERANDAH

RAFFLES HOTEL, SINGAPORE.

"The Savoy of Singapore."—*The London Sphere.*

Acknowledged to be by far the Best in the Straits Settlements. 🎔 🎔 🎔

THIS Hotel is a building of noble proportions and imposing appearance. It commands an area of over 200,000 square feet and faces the Sea, has a commanding view of the Harbour, and the adjacent Islands. Is close to all the Government Offices, Banks, Post and Telegraph Office and the Mercantile Quarters; whilst that which may well recommend it most to the weary traveller arriving from a long sea voyage is its home comforts, which may best be attested by the records of its visitors' books, proving that some of the most distinguished Royalty and European personages have often made use of the Raffles Hotel whilst sojourning in Singapore.

The Hotel has over 150 rooms en suite

Club in Baltimore." The culinary team was fully in place the following month when the hotel engaged the services of "a specialist for Indian and Malay Curries and Sambals which will be served daily ... Special Curry Tiffins with sambals every Sunday at 1 pm."

And so began a decade of daily dining and special entertainment that elevated Raffles Hotel to traveller's landmark. The special dinner parties in particular caught the fancy of the public and were chronicled in great detail in *The Straits Times*.

At a Criterion Dinner held on 30 June 1902, some 250 guests were seated "at the numerous tables, and at every one the floral and other decorations were in the most charming taste, and the attendance was prompt and excellent. The menu was all that could be desired. The hot dishes were hot and the cold ones were cold ... the menus were most tasteful works of art. Indeed they were all taken away by the guests as charming souvenirs of a very pleasing occasion." The influence of the French chefs is evident from the menu: Canapés Modernes and Mock Turtle Soup followed by Rouget à la Reine Alexandra, Crème de Volaille à la Régence, Tournedos à la Chartreuse, Pâté de Foie Gras en Aspic, Selle de Mouton d'Australie à la Jardinière, Dindon Truffé au Jambon et Salade, and Asperges en Branche. For dessert, Mince Pies and Glace à la Roi Edward VII were served.

Equally impressive was the dinner staged "for gourmets and gourmands alike" on 12 January 1903 for the Russian Grand Duke Cyril. "It was the best from a gastronomical standpoint ever put on a public table in these latitudes ... It is easy to imagine the management of the Hotel feeling proud and haughty over their success; and it should be explained that apart from all details of menu, band and attendance, every table was a mass of fresh roses. There never was such a pretty show in Singapore," reported *The Straits Times*.

To improve standards, a "magnificent new kitchen, with mammoth patent French ranges, each nearly thirty feet long", opened in 1904. "It would take a poetic chef to describe the attractions of the new one now completed, which is undoubtedly the finest in the East," the press recounted, continuing:

"It is an immense gaily lighted airy apartment about 40 feet square and over 30 feet high, with the two vast ranges aforementioned. On either side of this epicurean hall, there are two rooms, each nearly half as large as the kitchen, which will be used as store room, pastry room, scullery and cold storage room respectively. The average hotel guest rarely sees the kitchen, but this is worth a visit. In a special block close by Mr Sarkies has built special quarters for his French chefs, and a ten-foot covered way leads from the kitchen to the anteroom beside the dining hall, where the dishes and plates are kept hot by steam during meal hours. Everything in this department is as neat as a new pin."

The first major event that tested the new kitchens was the Race Day dinner held on 30 April 1904:

"Raffles Hotel has long been one of the acknowledged show places of Singapore and during the past week it has outvied even its own previous successes in the way of catering. The race dinners have proved exceptionally good, and at the last of the series on Saturday evening the big Hotel dining room was filled with those who having spent the day at the race course were determined to end a delightful day pleasantly ... Indeed it must have been a dull dog whose gloomiest reflections were not chased away by the pleasure of the table and of the society at Raffles. A mellowing influence was at work under the rays of the electric lights and even the sober sided waiters appeared to spring around with a jaunty readiness which made the attendance seem a pleasure instead of a labour. Most of the tables had their quota of guests when the

*Postcards (left) and photographs
of the famous and the unknown
(above) are displayed in the
hotel's museum, as are the early
Dining Room and verandah views
(preceding pages).*

dinner started, and an excellent menu was presented. Electric fans kept the atmosphere beautifully cool while the music of the Town and Volunteer Club. As usual all nationalities were represented in the dining room and on Saturday there was a large number of well known faces there. The wines were in fine condition and altogether it was only a hypochondriac or a misanthrope who could not have relaxed amid such surroundings and none of these tribes were present. Every guest seemed to be under the special care of the argus-eyed management, with the result that a wish was met almost before it had been formulated. Certainly a thoroughly enjoyable evening can be spent at the Raffles."

On a typical Saturday in 1906 several of the hotels made special efforts to please their guests including the newly reconstructed Hotel de L'Europe which was Raffles' main rival until it closed in 1933. At Raffles "there was an excellent menu at tifffin and this drew a large number of guests. For dinner, the chef was again put upon his mettle and served up a menu that could not have been beaten by any of the first class restaurants in London. The dining hall was crowded the entire evening and many kind things were said about the management."

Just as Kipling's praise was to remain imbedded in the minds of travellers for generations, so too were the words of *The Sphere*, a popular London magazine, which in 1905 called Raffles "the Savoy of Singapore". The Savoy was the first hotel in Britain to maintain a world-class restaurant and the first anywhere to offer conveniences

taken for granted all over the world today. Under the guidance of the famous hotelier, César Ritz, and his equally famous chef, Auguste Escoffier, the hotel became synonymous with comfort, cuisine and service. Even today fine dining remains firmly based on the concepts and principles he perfected a century ago.

We shall never know if Tigran Sarkies met Ritz, who opened his Paris hotel of the same name in 1898, but undoubtedly the two were kindred spirits. Tigran Sarkies passed thousands of travellers through his hands with unfailing urbanity until his death in 1912, and introduced a new standard of style and luxury into Eastern hotels.

The novelty of Raffles' fancy dinners gradually wore off and by 1910 the press reports stop. Still, changes in the restaurants and kitchens were considered newsworthy and duly chronicled. In 1913, the year Raffles advertised as "the hotel that has made Singapore famous to tourists" and "the rendezvous of planters", a new bakery was opened "where excellent bread is being turned out under the hand of a capable European baker"

The hotel's food operations continued to expand. By 1918 Raffles was "the only hotel in the Straits Settlements with its own refreshment-room on the premises, with all novelties in confectionery, its own bakery ... its own internal ice and cold storage plan, and its own slaughter house — away from the hotel of course — at which the animals are killed and then sent to cold storage in the hotel refrigerators," it was recorded in the encyclopaedic tome *Present Day Impressions of the Far East*.

The creator of the Singapore Sling, Ngiam Tong Boon (above). Long Bar Steakhouse (left) serves quality cuts with Asian condiments.

The 1920s, a decade of growth and optimism in Singapore's hotel industry, saw several new additions to Raffles' food establishments with the opening of the Grill Room, the Raffles Cafe and the Ballroom.

The Grill Room was created in the Main Dining Room's large private dining alcove overlooking the Palm Court (where the Raffles Grill is today). Service was available from 8 am to midnight daily and "modern appointments, electric heaters, etc, have been introduced to ensure the needs of guests being promptly and efficiently met." Edward Wasserman, a traveller who dined at Raffles in the 1930s, recorded in *Velvet Voyaging*:

"We motored in a car of Cook's to the Raffles Hotel; here, I thought, was the East that Maugham, Sir Hugh Clifford, Bruce Lockhart and countless others have written about ... In the Grill Room and restaurant, for the first time, I met with large menus, with each item numbered, so that one ordered by number and not by name; and very often, may I add, by pointing. The Malaysian waiters speak little or no English, and one had a sense of curiosity as to what they really were thinking of when they went pattering off on their bare feet to bring in some dish they would never eat themselves."

The Raffles Cafe, a precursor of the modern hotel coffee shop, was located on the ground floor of the Bras Basah wing. "In that popular rendezvous are obtainable at all hours meals or refreshments of every kind. The alluring assortments of cakes, pastries and confections displayed there are the product of the hotel's own bakery, whence, besides the hotel requirements, daily deliveries of bread are made to outside customers," reported the 1923 edition of *Seaports of the Far East*.

But it was the opening of the "coolest ballroom in the East" and its famed Long Bar that set the mood for the two decades that preceded World War II. Whiskey stengahs, gin slings and Million Dollar cocktails were consumed in great quantities as guests sat in rattan chairs under whirring fans, listening to the hotel band and observing the flotsam and jetsam of the port city — rubber planters and tin miners, British colonial servants and commercial carpetbaggers, Australian and English husband-hunters and ladies of uncertain origins. "At the Raffles, a bottle of sparkling wine is waiting and perhaps there will be some one on the veranda who will join me and hear my tale," mused a traveller in the 1920s. Between the tea dances and formal dinner dances, Raffles management also organised cruise dinners for the large groups circumnavigating the globe who arrived during the tourist season, from January through March.

A typical day for a Raffles' resident circa 1920 up to the 1950s commenced with *chota hadjrie*, an Indian term for early breakfast, that was served in the rooms from 6 am to 8 am. The Main Dining Room offered breakfast from 9 am, lunch at 1 pm and dinner from 7:30 pm according to the menu. Meals and snacks at odd hours or taken in a hurry could be consumed in Raffles Cafe or the Grill Room. The Sunday tiffin was

A popular venue for imbibing: the Bar and Billiard Room (above). Dining al fresco in Raffles Courtyard (right) is always a pleasure in Singapore's tropical weather.

part and parcel of colonial social life. Tiffin, the Anglo-Indian word for lunch, is thought to be derived from an 18th-century English slang term for sipping. Daily tiffin could be either light or heavy but the Sunday tiffin buffet remained an occasion for over-indulgence, with mulligatawny, several curries and rice, oxtail stew, roast beef and Yorkshire pudding, all washed down with iced beer and pudding. This was followed by an almost obligatory long snooze.

Unfortunately very little is known about the staff who so diligently ran the kitchens and served the public during these years. We know that supervision of the kitchens continued to be in the hands of European chefs whilst, from the 1920s, the ranks were filled by Hainanese "cook boys". The Hainanese began their culinary training in the homes of 19th-century colonial employers and their clubs. As they laboured to produce English food they acquired some innovative techniques, becoming especially adept at using condiments such as tomato sauce, Worcestershire sauce and HP to flavour meat dishes.

As the hotel business flourished, and fathers brought in sons, uncles their nephews, Raffles became a Hainanese stronghold. This was perhaps most obvious in the bar. In a yellowed staff list dated 1955, found amongst old files dunng the 1989-1991 restoration, 24 of the 30-strong bar staff were Ngiams, Ngiam being a common Hainanese surname.

The staff list also revealed the astonishing long service of some of these people. Bar boy Ngiam Fock Juan served over 37 years, having joined in 1918. Heading the staff of 30 cooks was Tan Kwang Tong who had served 25 years. Cheong Tuck Choy, the Roast Cook, served 27 years while Soup Cook Leong Chin Lim had served 32 years. In the Dining Room, where the all-male staff was divided into Table Boys and *Tukang Ayers*, the equivalent of today's bus boys, Tan Pow Chew, Head Boy No 2, served 40 years, having joined in 1915, while *Tukang Ayer* No 1, Lim See Yap, served almost 41 years.

One of the biggest post-World War II changes was the transformation of the Grill Room into the Elizabethan Grill, in honour of the coronation of Queen Elizabeth II. The walls were panelled in dark oak, ceilings lowered and spanned with Tudor-style beams and English crests hung at intervals around the room. It was Singapore's first air-conditioned restaurant.

In fact, the air-conditioned Elizabethan Grill easily eclipsed the vast Main Dining Room which had remained virtually unchanged in appearance since its opening at the beginning of the century. The lengthy, highly eclectic menu had also remained virtually unchanged for a quarter century, from the early 1950s until the mid-1970s. Main dishes included Australian fillet steak and local grilled *ikan kurau*, wiener schnitzel, veal piccata, delice of duckling Espagnol, roast turkey à l'anglaise, Canadian salmon, fillets of Iceland plaice, baked herring, supreme of chicken Maryland, pheasant Orloff, beef Stroganoff, and chicken Mancinia. Soups included borscht, mulligatawny, minestrone, vichyssoise and French onion. The only Asian items on the menu, however, were chicken and prawn curries.

The gradual decline in Raffles Hotel's fortunes from the 1960s onwards coincided with the appearance of Orchard

Formal private dining in the Sarkie's Suite (top). A collection of memorabilia that includes the Singapore Sling glass, menus, brochures and the hotel's very own curry powder (left).

Road's first generation of international-style five-star hotels. These modern architectural wonders, with their vast lobbies and luxurious appointments, set new standards in comfort and drew into even sharper contrast the antiquated facilities of Singapore's Grand Old Lady.

Those who did sign their names in Raffles' register were now travellers in search of the past, and the Singapore of rubber planters and Somerset Maugham's short stories. Many more — from young backpackers and famous writers to Japanese and Australian tourists and World War II veterans — came simply to see, and spend a few hours enjoying a Singapore Sling and taking the obligatory photograph or two. To these nostalgia seekers, the hotel's shortcomings, including her notoriously unpredictable food, were deemed to be part of her charm. In response to the increased interest in Raffles' history, some efforts were made at revitalisation in the 1970s and early 1980s. The old Main Dining Room, for example, was rechristened the Tiffin Room and a menu introduced that included more "local" dishes. The Elizabethan Grill bar area was renamed the Writer's Bar in honour of the hotel's longstanding literary connections.

But to even the most sympathetic fan, it was all too obvious that no amount of nostalgic goodwill could compensate for the decrepit state of the hotel's aging facilities. Several restoration and redevelopment schemes, including adding highrise blocks, were proposed in the 1980s, while at one stage rumours of impending destruction attracted international press attention.

But the demolition rumours proved unfounded and in 1987 the hotel was gazetted a National Monument. Soon after, plans were revealed for the faithful restoration of the historic buildings to their circa 1915 appearance. Proposals for adding a high-rise tower were, happily, rejected in favour of a low-rise, architecturally similar extension interspersed with tropical gardens. Thus, in March 1989, Raffles closed her doors for the first time in over a century. And so they remained for two-and-a-half years.

In September 1991, the Grand Old Lady reappeared, her facade once again ablaze with lights, marking her redebut with a truly memorable party for 800 guests. Welcoming the guests was the Board of Raffles Hotel (1886) Pte Ltd including Executive Director Richard Helfer. Mr Helfer had carefully guided Raffles' rebirth, not only working closely with architects and designers at every stage but conceptualising the new hotel in all its details, including restaurants. And all the while conscious of the hotel's role in history.

Today, Raffles Hotel is infused with new life in a manner that honours the past as much as it salutes the present. With only 104 suites (including the seven Grand Hotel Suites and ten Personality Suites), Raffles is like a stately home where guests are treated as residents and pampered in an atmosphere of privacy and intimacy. Redecorated to wonderfully comfortable standards, all the traditional Raffles touches remain intact: lushly planted gardens, spacious, beautifully appointed suites, shady verandahs, polished timber floors, high ceilings and whirring ceiling fans.

Old kopi tiam furniture (top) and wooden doors (right) give the Empire Cafe and the adjoining Ah Teng's Bakery a relaxed, cosy old-world charm.

The range of cuisines is decidedly Raffles, from the fine French food with a light, modern touch served in the Raffles Grill and the sumptuous, spicy curry tiffin served buffet style in the Tiffin Room, to the delicious local hawker-style dishes of Empire Cafe, the tasty treats from Ah Teng's Bakery, the delicious Cantonese cuisine of the Empress Room and the cutting-edge transethnic fusion of Doc Cheng's. It is the signature recipes of these restaurants which are shared in the pages that follow.

No introduction to Raffles' new food traditions would be complete, however, without mention of her other restaurants, bars, and function rooms. There is, for example, casual dining in the always lively Seah Street Deli, a New York-style deli offering enormous sandwiches and a truly outstanding cheesecake, and Raffles Courtyard, where the hotel's tradition of dining *al fresco* continues. Then there are two of the hotel's most historic venues, the Bar and Billiard Room and the Long Bar. Having been handsomely restored, billiard tables and all, the Bar and Billiard Room serves a delicious daily luncheon buffet. In the evening it becomes a connoisseur's haven, with cabinets of the world's finest cigars, spirits — malts, cognacs, armagnacs, ports, cigars, champagnes — coffees and chocolates. The Long Bar, where the Singapore Sling still reigns supreme, attracts a fascinating clientele. In the Long Bar Steakhouse, top quality meats are marinated with exotic Asian spices and cooked to perfection.

Not surprisingly, Raffles Hotel is also the setting for some of the best parties in town. The Ballroom is in demand for celebrations of all kinds, as are the East India Rooms, which are located in the oldest part of the hotel, and the Casuarina Suites, named after Somerset Maugham's famous volume of Asian short stories, *The Casuarina Tree*.

The hotel takes every advantage of Singapore's position as one of the air crossroads of the world to source the best products which are airflown in daily — strawberries from the United States, milk from Australia, abalone and scallops from Japan, salmon from Norway, Angus beef from Scotland, lobster from South Africa and herbs, salad greens and vegetables from France.

Exacting standards prevail. Fresh food is purchased daily as the hotel does not maintain a perishable store. Between 9 am and 11 am, the receiving dock is like a bustling market. Here the chefs check and receive, reject and complain. The ingredients are distributed to the hotel's numerous kitchens, where the skill and artistry of the chefs take over. Then from the kitchens to the tables. Meals are served with attention in elegant historic surroundings. Proud of the hotel's heritage and unique standing, and determined that each and every guest have the best, the staff daily conspire to make dining a truly memorable affair.

Thos SB Raffles (above), purveyor of fine food and wine. A waiter (right) serves breakfast on the Palm Court Verandah. The Raffles Courtyard's tapas bar (following pages).

Chapter One

THE RAFFLES GRILL

hen the Main Building opened in 1899, the entire ground floor was devoted to dining. The Main Dining Room boasted cool marble floors, tall French doors, ceiling fans, elegant appointments and was "capable of seating 500". At the turn of the century there was no dining room more handsome in the East.

In 1923, a portion of the Main Dining Room facing the Palm Court was set aside as a Grill Room "to answer what is undoubtedly a pressing need" according to a newspaper report of the day. In the early 1950s the room was altered once again, this time undergoing redecoration in Tudor style for rechristening as the Elizabethan Grill in honour of the coronation of Queen Elizabeth II.

Elegant and formal, Raffles Grill now looks much as it did when the management first invited diners to "book tables early to avoid disappointment". With its classical detailing beautifully restored and French windows once again overlooking the Palm Court, the room conveys a sense of timeless grace. The service is attentive yet discreet. Here the traditional art of gracious hospitality has been perfected.

The cuisine, however, has been unabashedly updated to suit today's demanding gourmets. Light and simple yet imaginative and original, the cooking style is rooted in the French classical tradition, with contemporary overtones.

The kitchen is in the hands of Chef de Cuisine David Mollicone and his highly skilled and dedicated team. Their starting point is the sourcing of the finest ingredients available anywhere in the world. Among the foods especially flown in are exquisite French truffles, fresh Scottish King scallops and the best Italian olive oils. Local items, especially seafood and vegetables, are incorporated into the dishes wherever applicable. While the influence of the South of France is unmistakable in the flavours, an Asian twist can be detected in the subtle and fascinating seasonings of some of the dishes.

Raffles Grill also prides itself on its celebrated wine cellar. To the traditional sources of France, Italy and Germany have been added outstanding vintages from newer wine regions such as California, Australia, New Zealand and South Africa.

Thus dining at Raffles Grill is a truly delightful experience that is long remembered.

Raffles Grill in a quiet moment as it awaits the arrival of luncheon guests.

Saumon fumé à chaud
(HOT-SMOKED ATLANTIC SALMON)

Serves 4

Chicken Stock

1.8 kg	Chicken bones, blanched
2.9 L	Water
80 g	Carrots, medium-diced
80 g	Onions, medium-diced
60 g	Celery, medium-diced
10 g	Garlic cloves
1 sprig	Parsley
1	Bay leaf
1 sprig	Thyme
10	Black peppercorn
2	Cloves
	Salt

(Mirepoix: Carrots, Onions, Celery, Garlic cloves)

Hot-Smoked Atlantic Salmon

60 g	Hickory wood chips, soaked for at least 1 hour
400 g	Fresh salmon fillet
20 mL	Corn oil
2 tsp	Salt
	Freshly ground white pepper

Potatoes

4	New potatoes
500 mL	Chicken stock
	Salt
	Freshly ground white pepper

Salad

60 g	Lollo rosso lettuce
60 g	Red oak leaf lettuce
60 g	Raddichio
60 g	Frisée
40 g	Arugula
20 g	Chives
20 g	Chervil
30 g	Bean sprouts
30 g	Yellow frisée
20 g	Tarragon
30 g	Beetroot leaves
30 g	Celery leaves
30 g	Watercress

Herb Vinaigrette

1	Shallot, finely chopped
30 g	Italian parsley, julienned
2 tbsp	Red vinegar
4 tbsp	Olive oil
	Salt
	Freshly ground black pepper

Garnish

60 g	Raffles Sevruga caviar
4 tbsp	Sour cream
	Sea salt

PREPARATION AND PRESENTATION

1. **Chicken stock**

   Rinse the chicken bones and combine them with the water in a pot. Bring to a boil over low heat, then reduce the heat and simmer for 4 to 5 hours, skimming from time to time.

   Add the mirepoix, herbs and spices in the last hour of simmering. Season to taste and pass the mixture through a fine sieve.

2. **Hot-smoked Atlantic salmon**

   Coat both sides of the salmon fillet with corn oil to prevent from drying and the skin from sticking to the pan while smoking. Season well with salt and pepper. Place the salmon fillet on a baking sheet or suitable pan. Remove the wood chips from the water, drain and arrange them in the bottom of the smoker.

   Place the pan on the shelf. Place the smoker on a hot plate or gas burner on low heat, just enough to make the wood chips smoke but not burn. Turn off the heat and keep the smoker closed for approximately 30 minutes until the flesh is slightly firm and has a shiny, pink colour. It should be slightly undercooked but not raw, in order to retain its natural moisture and flavour. Keep warm until used.

3. **Potatoes**

   Peel the potatoes lengthwise as evenly as possible. Keep them in cold water to prevent discolouring. Season the chicken stock and bring to a boil. Add the potatoes and simmer for 10 minutes or until done. Remove the pot from the heat but leave the potatoes in the stock as they will be served warm.

4. **Salad**

   Wash and pat dry all the lettuce leaves. Tear them into slightly larger than bite-sized pieces. Cover with a damp cloth and keep cool.

5. **Herb vinaigrette**

   Combine all the herb vinaigrette ingredients. Season to taste, mix well and set aside.

6. **To finish and serve**

   Remove the potatoes from the pot and slice them evenly. Toss the lettuce greens in the herb vinaigrette, then arrange them on 4 plates with the potatoes. Spoon the caviar and sour cream on the side as shown. Cut the salmon into 4 equal portions and remove the skin, leaving a strip at one end of each portion. Arrange the salmon next to the salad and potatoes. Sprinkle some sea salt over. Spoon the remaining herb vinaigrette on the side. Serve immediately, while the salmon is still warm.

Chef's Notes

– Wood chips from cherry, pear, apple, chestnut and olive trees are excellent for smoking. Avoid using pine tree chips as they are too acidic and have a high resin content.

– The Riesling, with aromas of lemon and spice, is the perfect complement for the smoked salmon.

Hot-Smoked Atlantic Salmon.

ℛAFFLES CAVIAR WITH BLINIS

Special equipment: 2 non-stick frying pans of 7-cm diameter

Serves 4

Raffles Caviar

120 g	Raffles Oscietre Golden caviar
70 g	Crème fraîche
70 g	Échiré butter

Blinis

2	Eggs
2 tbsp	Milk
1 tbsp	Yeast
100 g	Buckwheat flour, sifted
30 g	Caster sugar
30 g	Butter
2 tbsp	Vegetable oil
	Salt

PREPARATION AND PRESENTATION

1. Blinis

   Separate the egg yolks from the whites.
   In a small pan, warm the milk and mix in the yeast.
   Combine this mixture with the egg yolks and mix well.
   Fold in the buckwheat flour and season to taste.
   Whisk the egg whites with the sugar until the mixture is stiff, then fold it into the batter.
   Melt the butter over medium heat until golden brown. Add it to the batter and mix well.
   Warm the vegetable oil in the non-stick frying pans and spoon the batter over.
   Pan-fry the blinis on both sides until golden brown.

2. To finish and serve

   Serve the caviar on ice with warm blinis, crème fraîche and Échiré butter on the side.

Chef's Note

– Caviar is best enjoyed with mother-of-pearl or ivory spoons because the natural materials do not modify the caviar's original taste and serving temperature.

– Fine vintage Champagne will emphasise the caviar's exquisite taste.

Raffles Caviar with Blinis, Crème Fraîche and Échiré Butter.

CARRÉ ET SELLE DE PORCELET
(CRISPY RACK AND SADDLE OF SUCKLING PIG)

Serves 4

Suckling Pig

2	Racks of suckling pig
1	Saddle of suckling pig
6	Bay leaves
6 sprigs	Thyme
50 mL	Clarified butter
30 g	Salt
	Freshly ground black pepper

Marjoram Jus

250 g	Pig's trimmings
50 mL	Oil
30 g	Onions, medium-diced
30 g	Carrots, medium-diced
30 g	Leek, medium-diced
2	Apples, medium-diced
30 g	Garlic cloves
4	Pig's trotters
20 mL	Port wine
1 L	Water
3	Bay leaves
5 sprigs	Thyme
20 g	Marjoram
	Salt
	Freshly ground black pepper

Vegetable Fricassée

30 g	Baby leek
30 g	Baby turnips
30 g	Baby carrots
100 g	Tomato concassée
20 g	Butter
30 g	Chervil
30 g	Salt
	Freshly ground black pepper

Garnish

20 g	Marjoram

PREPARATION AND PRESENTATION

1. Suckling pig
   Preheat the oven to 190°C.
   Season the bone side of the suckling pig's racks and saddle with salt, pepper, bay leaves and thyme.
   Brush the skin with clarified butter.
   Bake in the oven for approximately 40 minutes or until the skin is crispy.

2. Marjoram jus
   In a large saucepan, pan-fry the pig's trimmings until golden brown, then add the vegetables and fruit, and sauté for a further 6 minutes.
   Add the pig's trotters, port wine and water.
   Season to taste and simmer for 1^1/$_2$ hours.
   Remove the pig's trotters from the stock and separate the meat from the bones. Chop the meat and set aside.
   Pass the stock through a fine sieve. Reduce it by half, then add the meat and marjoram.
   Season to taste and mix well.

3. Vegetable fricassée
   Cook all the vegetables separately in salted boiling water, then toss them in the butter and chervil.
   Season to taste.

4. To finish and serve
   Remove excess salt from the suckling pig. Cut its racks into pieces and the saddle into 4 equal portions.
   Arrange the racks with some vegetables in the centre of each plate.
   Place some of the remaining vegetables on 1 side and the saddle on the other.
   Spoon the sauce over and garnish with the marjoram.
   Serve immediately.

Chef's Notes

− If the suckling pig's skin is not crispy enough, place it under a salamander for 8 − 10 minutes.
− Wrap the racks of suckling pig in aluminium foil to prevent them from burning during the baking process.
− The Pinot Noir's silky tannins will harmonise with the crisp flavours of the suckling pig.

Crispy Rack and Saddle of Suckling Pig.

APPETIZERS

Soupe Paysanne de Légumes et Couteaux de Mer
(MINESTRONE OF VEGETABLES AND BAMBOO CLAMS)

Special equipment: Electric hand-held blender

Serves 4

Fish Stock

60 mL	Oil
2.5 kg	Fish bones
80 g	Carrots, medium-diced
80 g	Onions, medium-diced
60 g	Celery, medium-diced
10 g	Garlic cloves
140 g	Mushroom trimmings
2.4 L	Water
500 mL	Dry white wine
1 sprig	Parsley
1	Bay leaf
1 sprig	Thyme
10	Black peppercorns
2	Cloves
	Salt

(Carrots, Onions, Celery, Garlic cloves } Mirepoix)

Fish Soup

50 mL	Olive oil
30 g	Bayonne ham, sliced
20 g	Garlic cloves
50 g	Sweet onions, quartered
200 g	Savoy cabbage, diced
100 g	Cauliflower, diced
100 g	Potatoes, diced
30 g	Leeks, diced
30 g	Carrots, diced
30 g	Turnips, diced
5	Bay leaves
5 sprigs	Thyme
250 mL	Dry white wine
1 L	Fish stock
	Salt
	Freshly ground black pepper

Bamboo Clams

6 - 8	Bamboo clams

Garnish

100 g	Green cabbage leaves, cooked and puréed in a blender
30 g	Fava beans, cooked in salted boiling water
30 g	Green beans, cooked in salted boiling water
1 tbsp	Truffle oil
50 mL	Olive oil
20 mL	Armagnac
	Salt
	Freshly ground black pepper

PREPARATION AND PRESENTATION

1. Fish stock

   Heat the oil in a stockpot and sweat the fish bones and mirepoix. Add the mushroom trimmings and toss well. Add the water, white wine, herbs and spices, and bring to a simmer. Simmer for 35 to 40 minutes, skimming from time to time.

   Season to taste. Pass the mixture through a fine sieve.

2. Fish soup

   In a pot, heat the olive oil and sauté the ham, garlic and onions for 4 minutes.

   Add all the vegetables and herbs, and sauté for 10 minutes over low heat.

   Deglaze with the white wine and simmer for 10 minutes to reduce the liquid. This process also eliminates the alcohol from the wine.

   Add the fish stock and season to taste.

   Simmer for 40 minutes. Separate the solid ingredients from the soup and pass the soup through a fine sieve.

3. Bamboo clams

   Quickly poach the bamboo clams in the remaining fish stock, then separate the clams from the shells.

   Cut each shell into half and set aside for garnishing. Clean the clams and set aside.

4. To finish and serve

   Prepare 4 soup bowls. Heat the green cabbage purée in a saucepan. Using the back of a tablespoon, draw a strip of purée on the side of each soup bowl as shown.

   Warm the fava and green beans in the soup.

   Arrange the beans, solid ingredients from the soup, clams and clam shells in the bowls as shown.

   Season the soup to taste and process with a hand-held blender until foamy.

   Pour the soup into the bowls and drizzle the truffle oil, olive oil and Armagnac over. Serve immediately.

Chef's Notes

– Do not overcook the clams or they will become rubbery and lose their delicate flavour.

– Vegetarians may replace the fish stock with vegetable stock and the seafood with rice.

– A full-bodied wine like the Chardonnay will hold its ground against the soup's intense flavours superbly.

Minestrone of Vegetables and Bamboo Clams.

$\mathcal{E}$SCALOPE DE FOIE GRAS POËLÉ À L'UNILATÉRAL (DUCK LIVER PAN-SEARED ON ONE SIDE)

Special equipment: Mandoline and electric blender

Serves 4

Lemon Confit

2	Lemons
100 g	Sugar
300 mL	Water

Court Bouillon of Vegetables

650 g	Assorted mushrooms
30 g	Dried wild mushrooms
70 g	Celery, medium-diced
40 g	Leeks, medium-diced
15 g	Shallots
1.9 L	Water
15 mL	Vermouth
1 tsp	Thyme leaves
1 tsp	Chervil leaves
5	Juniper berries
1 tsp	Cracked black peppercorns
4	Garlic cloves
2	Bay leaves
1 tbsp	Olive oil

Pan-seared Duck Liver

4 slices	Duck liver (100 g each)
	Salt
	Freshly ground black pepper

Eggplant Salad

60 g	Butter
8	Eggplants, sliced
	Salt
	Freshly ground black pepper

Baby Eggplant Chips

1	Baby eggplant
200 mL	Vegetable oil
3 g	Salt

Black Olive Emulsion

100 g	Seedless black olives
200 mL	Court bouillon of vegetables
50 mL	Cream
50 mL	Olive oil
	Freshly ground black pepper

Salad

2 tbsp	Red wine vinegar
2 tbsp	Olive oil
60 g	Arugula leaves

Garnish

4 pcs	Semi-dried tomatoes (see recipe, pages 58 and 60)
4 tbsp	Yoghurt

PREPARATION AND PRESENTATION

1. Lemon confit
   Using a mandoline, cut the lemons into 0.2-cm-thick slices. Discard the ends.
   Combine the sugar and water in a pot and bring to a boil. Add the lemon slices and simmer for $1^{1}/_{2}$ hours. Remove the pot from the heat and set aside to cool. Keep refrigerated until used.

2. Court bouillon of vegetables
   Combine all the ingredients in a stockpot and bring to a simmer. Simmer for 45 minutes, skimming from time to time. Season to taste.
   Pass the mixture through a fine sieve.

3. Pan-seared duck liver
   Season the duck liver well with salt and pepper, then pan-fry the slices on only 1 side over low heat for 6 minutes until crispy and golden brown.
   Remove from the heat and place the duck liver on a plate lined with absorbent paper to remove the excess oil.

4. Eggplant salad
   In a frying pan, heat the butter and fry the eggplants on both sides until golden brown. Season to taste.

5. Baby eggplant chips
   Using the mandoline, cut the baby eggplant lengthwise into 0.1-cm-thick slices.
   Deep-fry in very hot oil for 3 minutes until crispy and golden brown. Remove the chips from the oil with a strainer and place them on a plate lined with absorbent paper to remove the excess oil.
   Sprinkle the salt over and set aside.
   Store in an airtight container until used.

6. Black olive emulsion
   Place the black olives and court bouillon in a pot and boil for 20 minutes.
   Process the mixture in the electric blender until smooth, then pour it into a pot and add the cream.
   Reduce the mixture by half over medium heat.
   Remove from the heat and pass it through a fine sieve.
   Add the olive oil and mix well.
   Season with pepper to taste.

7. Salad
   Mix the red wine vinegar and olive oil, and add to the arugula leaves. Toss well. You may add some cooking liquid from the duck liver to the salad.

8. To finish and serve
   Layer the eggplants and semi-dried tomatoes on 4 plates. Top each portion with duck liver slice and lemon confit. Top with a few arugula leaves and baby eggplant chips. Spoon some yoghurt on the side and top the yoghurt with some black olive emulsion to serve.

Chef's Notes

– The lemon confit can be kept refrigerated for up to 7 days.
– The Gewürztraminer's sweet and fruity flavour makes it the ideal accompaniment for the duck liver.

Duck Liver Pan-Seared On One Side.

$\mathscr{P}$OËLÉ DE CHAMPIGNONS, JUS BEURRÉ AUX NOISETTES
(WILD MUSHROOM FRICASSÉE WITH HAZELNUT JUS)

Special equipment: Electric blender

Serves 4

Chicken Jus

1.8 kg	Chicken bones, blanched	
60 mL	Oil	
2.9 L	Water	
80 g	Carrots, medium-diced	⎫
80 g	Onions, medium-diced	⎬ Mirepoix
60 g	Celery, medium-diced	⎪
10 g	Garlic cloves	⎭
60 mL	Tomato paste	
	Salt	

Wild Mushroom Fricassée

300 g	Cèpe mushrooms
150 g	Girolle mushrooms
150 g	Black trumpet mushrooms
4 tbsp	Olive oil
20 g	Garlic cloves
50 g	Butter
4 tbsp	Chicken jus
200 g	Spinach leaves
30 g	Italian parsley
100 mL	Heavy cream
5	Bay leaves

Hazelnut Jus

100 g	Hazelnuts
80 g	Butter
3 tbsp	Hazelnut oil
	Salt
	Freshly ground black pepper

Almond Purée

200 mL	Milk
200 mL	Cream
300 g	Whole almonds, peeled
10 g	Nutmeg, grated
	Salt
	Freshly ground black pepper

PREPARATION AND PRESENTATION

1. Chicken jus
   Rinse the chicken bones and dry them.
   In a roasting pan, brown them with the oil, then combine them with the water in a stockpot.
   Bring to a boil over low heat, then simmer for 4 hours, skimming from time to time.
   In the roasting pan, brown the mirepoix and tomato paste. Add this to the stock.
   Deglaze the pan with some water and add the mixture to the stock. Simmer for 1 hour. Season to taste.
   Pass the mixture through a fine sieve.

2. Wild mushroom fricassée
   Wash all the mushrooms, then pat them dry with kitchen tissue.
   Heat the olive oil in a frying pan and sauté the cèpe mushrooms until soft, then add the girolle mushrooms and garlic. Season to taste. Cook covered for 5 minutes.
   Add the butter and chicken jus, and cook covered for a further 2 minutes.
   Add the spinach and Italian parsley and toss well.
   In a separate pan, combine the heavy cream, black trumpet mushrooms and bay leaves.
   Simmer for 5 minutes until the mushrooms are cooked. Season to taste.

3. Hazelnut jus
   Sauté the hazelnuts in the butter until golden brown.
   Add the hazelnut oil and whisk to mix well.
   Add the cooking liquid from the sautéed cèpe mushrooms and mix well. Season to taste.

4. Almond purée
   Combine the milk, cream and almonds in a pot and bring to a boil.
   Reduce the heat and simmer for 20 minutes.
   Process the mixture in the electric blender on high speed until smooth.
   Add the nutmeg and mix well. Season to taste.

5. To finish and serve
   Prepare 4 plates. Place a spoonful of almond purée on each plate and top with the mushroom fricassée.
   Drizzle the hazelnut jus around and garnish with the roasted hazelnuts to serve.

Chef's Notes
- Dried mushrooms are not recommended for the dish.
- If cèpe, girolle or black trumpet mushrooms are not available, use other fresh seasonal mushrooms.
- The earthy flavours and meaty texture of the mushrooms are best complemented by the Chenin.

Wild Mushroom Fricassée with Hazelnut Jus.

ℒANGOUSTINES CUITES À CRU SUR UNE SALADE DE COURGETTES
(MARINATED SCAMPI WITH ZUCCHINI SALAD)

Serves 4

Marinated Scampi

12	Scampis
2 tbsp	Olive oil
	Juice from 1 lemon
	Salt
	Freshly ground black pepper

Tomato Confit with Port Wine

100 mL	Port wine, reduced by half
100 g	Tomato concassée
2	Tomatoes, quartered

Cream of Cod

200 g	Salted cod
2	Hard-boiled eggs, shelled
6 tbsp	Olive oil
100 mL	Cream
40 g	Garlic cloves
	Salt
	Freshly ground black pepper

Zucchini Salad

200 g	Zucchini
30 g	Green peas
1	Egg yolk
50 g	Black olives
20 g	Shallots
20 g	Parsley
60 g	Mixed salad leaves (baby cress, oak leaves, frisée, baby spinach and beetroot leaves)
3 tbsp	Avocado oil

Garnish

4 stalks	Chives, cut into 3-cm lengths

PREPARATION AND PRESENTATION

1. Marinated scampi
   Blanch the scampis in salted boiling water for 1 minute, then remove and refresh with iced water.
   Remove the shells and marinate the meat with the remaining ingredients.

2. Tomato confit with port wine
   Preheat the oven to 110°C. Combine the port wine reduction and tomato concassée in a bowl and toss well. Divide the mixture into 4 portions.
   Place the ring moulds on 4 plates and fill them with the tomato mixture.
   Top with the tomato quarters and bake in the oven for 1 hour until the tomatoes are soft and semi-dry.

3. Cream of cod
   Bake the salted cod in the oven preheated to 110 °C for 15 minutes (medium). Combine the fish with the remaining ingredients in a blender and process until smooth. Season to taste.

4. Zucchini salad
   Cut zucchini into pieces and blanch them together with the green peas in salted boiling water for 1 minute, then refresh with iced water.
   Combine them with all the remaining ingredients and toss well. Season to taste.

5. To finish and serve
   Prepare 4 plates. Place the zucchini in the centre of each plate and the tomato confit on the side.
   Remove the ring moulds from the tomato confit.
   Arrange the marinated scampi on top of the zucchini. Place a stick of chive on each scampi.
   Spoon some cream of cod on the side and garnish with the remaining salad leaves and green peas from the zucchini salad to serve.

Chef's Notes
- Serve the cream of cod as a dip with raw vegetable sticks.
- Avocado oil is available in gourmet supermarkets. If unavailable, replace it with olive oil or grapeseed oil.
- The refreshing acidity of the Sauvignon Blanc marries well with seafood.

Marinated Scampi with Zucchini Salad.

MAIN COURSES

DOS DE DORADE MEUNIÈRE EN COCOTTE D'ARTICHAUTS
(PAN-SEARED ROYAL SEA BREAM WITH ARTICHOKES)

Special equipment: Mandoline

Serves 4

Pan-Seared Royal Sea Bream

4	Sea breams (380 g each), cleaned and scaled
3 tbsp	Olive oil
5 sprigs	Thyme
	Salt
	Freshly ground black pepper

Garlic Confit

20	Garlic cloves, unpeeled
10 tbsp	Olive oil
5 tbsp	Water
5	Bay leaves
3 sprigs	Thyme
	Salt
	Freshly ground black pepper

Vegetables

100 g	Girolle mushrooms
16 stalks	Asparagus
8	Summer onions
4	Artichokes, trimmed and sliced thinly with the mandoline
40 g	Fava beans
4 tbsp	Olive oil
200 mL	Chicken stock (see recipe, page 40)
50 g	Butter
4	Bay leaves, chopped
4 cloves	Garlic confit
	Salt
	Freshly ground black pepper

Garnish

1	Lemon, thinly sliced and pan-fried until golden brown and semi-dry
80 g	Bayonne ham, baked in the oven preheated to 120°C for 15 minutes
30 g	Chives, cut into 4-cm lengths
100 mL	Chicken jus (see recipe, page 51)

PREPARATION AND PRESENTATION

1. Pan-seared royal sea bream
   Season the sea breams well with salt and pepper.
   In a pan, heat the olive oil and pan-fry the fish with the thyme over low heat for 4 - 5 minutes on each side (medium).

2. Garlic confit
   Blanch the garlic cloves in salted boiling water for 2 minutes, then refresh them with iced water.
   Peel the garlic and place them in a pot.
   Add the olive oil, water and herbs, and season to taste.
   Bring to a boil, then reduce the heat and simmer for 45 minutes over medium heat (approximately 85°C).
   Remove the garlic and reduce the liquid until the water evaporates completely.
   Glaze the garlic with the remaining oil.

3. Vegetables
   Cut the mushrooms into bite-sized pieces.
   Lightly sauté the mushrooms, vegetables and pulses in the olive oil and season to taste.
   Add the chicken stock and simmer until all the vegetables and pulses are tender. Strain and set aside.
   Reduce the cooking liquid by half, then whisk in the butter and bay leaves.
   Mash the garlic confit and add to the vegetables.
   Mix well and season to taste.

4. To finish and serve
   Cut off the sea breams' heads and place each in the corner of a square plate.
   Garnish with a slice of pan-fried lemon, bay leaves, mushrooms and fava beans.
   Debone the body and place a fillet on the left side of the plate. Garnish with the crispy ham.
   Arrange 4 stalks of asparagus on each plate as shown and place the other fillet on the asparagus.
   Garnish with the artichokes and chives and arrange some summer onions on the side.
   Spoon some chicken jus on the side to serve.

Chef's Notes
- Sea bream may be replaced with turbot, John Dory or cod.
- If Bayonne ham is unavailable, use Parma ham or bacon.
- A medium-bodied Tokay Pinot Gris, with spicy character and fruity notes, is the perfect wine for this dish.

Pan-Seared Royal Sea Bream with Artichokes.

Poitrine de Pigeon Pochée aux Agrumes Epicées
(POACHED PIGEON BREAST WITH SPICY CITRUS CONSOMMÉ)

Special equipment: 4 ring moulds of 10-cm diameter and 2.5-cm depth

Serves 4

Pigeon Stock

4	Pigeons (450 g each)
60 mL	Oil
2.9 L	Water
80 g	Carrots, medium-diced
80 g	Onions, medium-diced
60 g	Celery, medium-diced
10 g	Garlic cloves
90 mL	Tomato paste
1 sprig	Parsley
1	Bay leaf
1 sprig	Thyme
10	Black peppercorns
2	Cloves
	Salt

(Carrots, Onions, Celery, Garlic cloves = Mirepoix)

Poached Pigeon Breast

1 L	Pigeon stock
	Zest from 1 lemon, blanched
	Zest from 1/2 pomelo, blanched
	(reserve the segments for the sauce)
	Zest from 1 orange, blanched
	(reserve the segments for the sauce)

Shallot Confit

10	Shallots, unpeeled
10 tbsp	Olive oil
5 tbsp	Water
5	Bay leaves
3 sprigs	Thyme
	Salt
	Freshly ground black pepper

Crunchy Lobster Gateau

100 g	Leek, diced
100 g	Zucchini, diced
100 g	Spinach, blanched
4	Shallot confit
	Meat from 1 lobster, poached for 6 minutes in the pigeon stock and refreshed with iced water
10 g	Marjoram, chopped
30 g	Parsley, chopped
30 g	Mint, chopped
30 g	Thai basil, chopped
4 sheets	Brick pastry
1	Egg yolk, beaten
2 tbsp	Olive oil
	Salt
	Freshly ground black pepper

Vegetables

4	Vine-ripened tomatoes
4 tbsp	Olive oil
8 stalks	Celery
	Salt
	Freshly ground black pepper

Cardamom Jus

100 mL	Pigeon stock
	Juice from 2 calamansi limes
20 mL	Grapeseed oil
5	Cardamom seeds
1 tbsp	Pomelo sacs

Garnish

4	Lobster claws, poached for 6 minutes in the pigeon stock, shelled and sautéed in olive oil
4 cloves	Garlic confit (see recipe, page 54)
4 slices	Lemon confit (see recipe, page 48)

PREPARATION AND PRESENTATION

1. Pigeon stock
   Debone the pigeons and set the breasts and legs aside.
   Rinse the bones and dry them.
   In a roasting pan, brown them with the oil, then combine them with the water in a stockpot.
   Bring to a boil over low heat, then simmer for 5 hours, skimming from time to time.
   In the roasting pan, brown the mirepoix and tomato paste. Add this to the stock.
   Deglaze the pan with some water and add the mixture to the stock. Add the herbs and spices, and season to taste. Simmer for 1 hour.
   Pass the mixture through a fine sieve.

2. Poached pigeon breast
   Infuse the citrus zest in the pigeon stock and poach the pigeon breasts and legs in the stock for 7 minutes, without bringing to a boil.
   Remove the pigeons from the stock and set aside to rest for 15 minutes.
   Poach the pigeons in the stock again for 5 minutes, then debone the legs and return the meat to the stock.

3. Shallot confit
   Blanch the shallots in salted boiling water for 10 minutes, then refresh them with iced water.
   Peel the shallots and place them in a pot.
   Add the olive oil, water and herbs, and season to taste.
   Bring to a boil, then reduce the heat and simmer for 1 hour over medium heat (approximately 85°C).
   Remove the shallots and reduce the liquid until the water evaporates completely.
   Glaze the shallots with the remaining oil.

4. Crunchy lobster gateau
   Cook all the vegetables in salted boiling water until *al dente* (firm to the bite), then refresh them with iced water to retain their colour and texture.

Poached Pigeon Breast with Spicy Citrus Consommé.

Chop the shallot confit.

Add the shallot confit, the poached and diced lobster meat, and herbs to the vegetables.

Mix well and season to taste.

Divide the vegetable mixture into 4 portions and wrap each portion in a sheet of brick pastry.

Seal with egg wash and refrigerate for 30 minutes.

Pan-fry the gateau quickly in the olive oil, then bake them in the oven preheated to 180°C for 5 minutes until crispy and golden brown.

5. Vegetables

Preheat the oven to 170°C.

Season the tomatoes well with salt and pepper.

Drizzle the olive oil over and bake in the oven for 8 minutes. Carefully peel off the skin and set aside.

Remove the celery's fibres and cut each stalk into half.

Cook them in salted boiling water for 6 minutes. Set aside.

6. Cardamom jus

Combine all the ingredients, except the pomelo sacs and cardamom seeds, in a pan and reduce until it reaches a syrupy consistency. Add the pomelo sacs.

Roast the cardamom seeds in a pan and add them to the sauce. Mix well.

Pass the sauce through a fine sieve and season to taste.

7. To finish and serve

Arrange 4 pieces of celery in the centre of each plate as shown and glaze them with some cardamom jus.

Slice the pigeon meat and place them on the celery.

Place a lobster gateau, a lobster claw and a tomato next to each serving of pigeon.

Drizzle more cardamom jus around.

Garnish each plate with a garlic confit and a slice of lemon confit. Serve immediately.

Chef's Notes
- Cooking the pigeons in 2 steps ensures that the meat is tender.
- For a velvety finish on the palate, savour the pigeon with a glass of Merlot.

CÔTE DE VEAU RÔTIE ET RAVIOLES D'HERBES
(ROASTED MILK-FED RACK OF VEAL WITH SHEEP'S CHEESE AND HERB RAVIOLI)

Special equipment: Round-shaped dough cutter of 8-cm diameter and electric blender

Serves 4

Veal Stock

1.8 kg	Veal bones (including knuckles and trimmings)	
60 mL	Oil	
2.9 L	Water	
80 g	Carrots, medium-diced	
80 g	Onions, medium-diced	Mirepoix
60 g	Celery, medium-diced	
10 g	Garlic cloves	
90 mL	Tomato paste	
1 sprig	Parsley	
1	Bay leaf	
1 sprig	Thyme	
10	Black peppercorns	
2	Cloves	
	Salt	

Roasted Milk-Fed Rack of Veal

1.2 kg	Rack of veal
50 mL	Vegetable oil
5 sprigs	Thyme
5	Bay leaves
10	Garlic cloves, crushed
60 g	Butter
	Salt
	Freshly ground black pepper

Semi-Dried Tomatoes

2	Tomatoes
2 tbsp	Olive oil
2 cloves	Garlic, thinly sliced
2 sprigs	Thyme
	Salt
	Freshly ground black pepper

Pasta Dough

200 g	Gluten-enriched flour, sifted
2	Eggs
1 tbsp	Water
1 tbsp	Olive oil
2 g	Salt

Roasted Milk-Fed Rack of Veal with Sheep's Cheese and Herb Ravioli served on a silver trolley.

Sheep's Cheese and Herb Ravioli

100 g	Fresh sheep's cheese
50 g	Semi-dry sheep's cheese
12 cloves	Garlic confit (see recipe, page 54)
8 pcs	Semi-dried tomatoes
200 g	Silver beet, blanched and finely chopped
30 g	Parsley, chopped
50 mL	Olive oil
200 g	Pasta dough
3	Egg yolks, beaten
	Salt
	Freshly ground black pepper

Bay Leaf Butter

15	Bay leaves
2 sprigs	Rosemary
100 mL	Water
100 g	Butter
20 mL	Olive oil
	Salt
	Freshly ground black pepper

Vegetable Confit

30 g	Zucchini, finely diced
30 g	Eggplants, finely diced
30 g	Tomatoes, finely diced
10 g	Onions, finely diced
1	Garlic clove, crushed
1 tbsp	Olive oil
1 sprig	Thyme
1 sprig	Basil
500 mL	Veal stock
100 g	Tomato concassée

PREPARATION AND PRESENTATION

1. Veal stock

   Rinse the veal bones and dry them.
   In a roasting pan, brown them with the oil,
   then combine them with the water in a stockpot.
   Bring to a boil over low heat, then simmer for 5 hours, skimming from time to time.
   In the roasting pan, brown the mirepoix and tomato paste. Add this to the stock.
   Deglaze the pan with water and add the mixture to the stock. Add the herbs and spices.
   Season to taste and simmer for 1 hour.
   Pass the mixture through a fine sieve.

2. Roasted milk-fed rack of veal

   Preheat the oven to 190°C.
   Season the veal rack well with salt and pepper.
   Heat the vegetable oil in a frying pan and pan-sear the racks until light brown.
   Add the herbs, garlic and butter and bake for 1 hour, basting the racks every 10 minutes with the cooking fat.

3. Semi-dried tomatoes

   Preheat the oven to 120°C.
   Blanch the tomatoes in salted boiling water for 30 seconds, then refresh them with iced water.
   Peel the tomatoes, quarter them, then remove the seeds.
   Arrange the tomatoes on a baking tray (core facing upwards) and season to taste.
   Drizzle the olive oil over, then sprinkle the garlic and thyme over.
   Bake the tomatoes in the oven for 30 minutes.
   Remove from the heat and set aside to cool.

4. Pasta dough

   Place the flour in a mixing bowl.
   Form a well in the centre and add all the remaining ingredients to the well.
   Incorporate the ingredients with your fingers. Knead into a smooth dough, then shape the dough into a ball.
   Set aside to rest at room temperature for 30 minutes.
   Keep it covered with a damp cloth during this time to prevent it from drying.

5. Sheep's cheese and herb ravioli

   Combine all the ingredients, except the pasta dough and egg yolks, in a bowl and mix well. Season to taste.
   Roll out the pasta dough and prepare the ravioli wrappers by cutting the pasta dough with the round dough cutter.
   Spoon some of the filling in the centre of each piece of dough and cover with another, sealing the sides with egg wash.
   Cook the raviolis in salted boiling water until *al dente* (firm to the bite).

6. Bay leaf butter

   Combine the bay leaves, rosemary and water in a pot and simmer for 10 minutes to infuse the flavours.
   Process this mixture in the electric blender until smooth, then strain and reduce by half.
   Whisk in the butter and olive oil, and mix well.
   Season to taste.

7. Vegetable confit

   Sauté the zucchini, eggplants, tomatoes, onions, garlic and herbs in olive oil until tender.
   Combine the veal stock and tomato concassée in a pan and reduce by half.
   Add the sautéed vegetables, bay leaf butter, raviolis and cooking fat from the roasted racks of veal. Mix well.

8. To finish and serve

   Serve the veal rack on a carving board with the vegetable confit and raviolis on the side.
   Serve the sauce in a sauceboat.
   The meat should be carved in front of your guests.

Chef's Notes

– The semi-dried tomatoes may be prepared a day ahead. Just drizzle the oil over the tomatoes after baking and store them in an airtight container. Keep refrigerated until used.
– This dish is best enjoyed with the robust and intensely aromatic Cabernet Sauvignon.

LA DACQUOISE AU CHOCOLAT, SYROP AUX POIVRONS DOUX
(CHOCOLATE DACQUOISE WITH CANDIED CAPSICUM)

Special equipment: Ice cream machine and 4 ring moulds of 6-cm diameter and 3-cm depth

Candied Red Capsicum
1	Red capsicum
100 g	Sugar
50 mL	Water

Pinenut Dacquoise Sponge
62 g	Ground pinenuts
50 g	Icing sugar
12 g	Flour
60 mL	Egg whites
12 g	Sugar

Chocolate Mousse
150 mL	Dark chocolate
4	Egg yolks
40 g	Sugar
20 mL	Water
150 mL	Whipping cream

Chocolate Chip Tuile
12 g	Flour
62 g	Sugar
31 g	Chocolate chips
12 mL	Fresh orange juice
31 g	Butter, melted

Chocolate Sticks
60 g	Dark chocolate

Clotted Cream Ice Cream
250 mL	Whole milk
75 mL	Whipping cream
50 mL	Clotted cream
25 g	Glucose
25 g	Invert sugar
	Beans from ½ vanilla pod
30 g	Sugar
4	Egg yolks

Garnish
10 g	Cocoa powder
120 g	Raspberries
80 g	Redcurrants, dusted with sugar
8 sprigs	Thyme, dipped in syrup and dried in oven preheated to 120°C for 5 minutes
	Beans from 1 vanilla pod

PREPARATION AND PRESENTATION

1. Candied red capsicum

   Preheat the oven to 180°C. Bake the red capsicum in the oven for 30 minutes. Remove from the heat and set aside to cool. Remove the skin and seeds.
   Combine the capsicum, sugar and water in a saucepan and cook until all the liquid evaporates. Set aside.

2. Pinenut dacquoise sponge

   Preheat the oven to 200°C. Combine the ground pinenuts, icing sugar and flour in a bowl and mix well. Whip the egg whites and sugar into a meringue with a wooden spatula, then gently fold in the pinenut mixture. Spread the batter on a baking tray and bake in the oven for 8 minutes until the sponge is cooked and light brown. Remove from the heat and set aside to cool.

3. Chocolate mousse

   Melt the chocolate in a double boiler. Whisk the egg yolks for 5 minutes. Combine the sugar and water in a pot, and bring to a boil. Pour this mixture gently over the egg yolks and whisk for 5 minutes until fluffy. Whip the cream until light and fluffy, then fold it into the melted chocolate. Combine this with the egg yolk mixture and mix well. Cut 4 circles from the sponge with the ring moulds, then fill up the ring with chocolate mousse. Keep refrigerated until used.

4. Chocolate chip tuile

   Preheat the oven to 180°C. Combine all the dry ingredients in a bowl and mix well. Add the orange juice and butter, and mix well. Spread the batter thinly on a baking sheet and bake in the oven for 5 minutes until crispy and golden brown. Cut 4 strips, each measuring 20 by 2 cm. Roll each strip around the widest part of the wine bottle to form a ring. Set aside.

5. Chocolate sticks

   Melt the chocolate in a double boiler. Set aside to cool. Spread the chocolate thinly on a marble surface, then cut it into long sticks. Store in a cool place until used.

Chocolate Dacquoise with Candied Capsicum.

6. Clotted cream ice cream
   Combine all the ingredients, except the sugar and egg yolks, in a pan and bring to a boil. Whisk the sugar and egg yolks until creamy, then pour the hot cream mixture over, whisking continuously. Return the mixture to the pan and cook over medium heat for a further 2 minutes. Remove from the heat and pass the mixture through a fine sieve. Set aside to cool. Process in the ice cream machine as instructed.

7. To finish and serve
   Remove the chocolate dacquoise from the ring and dust them with cocoa powder. Place each portion on a plate. Garnish with the candied capsicum, a chocolate chip tuile, 2 chocolate sticks, 2 sprigs of thyme and some raspberries and redcurrants.
   Place a scoop of clotted cream ice cream on the side and sprinkle the vanilla beans over. Serve immediately.

Chef's Notes
– Relish this chocolate dessert with a glass of Muscat.

$\mathcal{A}$UTOUR DE LA POMME
(APPLE COMPOSITION)

Special equipment: Electric blender

Serves 4

Caramelised Apples

2	Apples, peeled and cored
80 g	Sugar

Sugar Crisp

40 g	Clarified butter
40 g	Icing sugar
30 g	Brown sugar
5 g	Cinnamon powder
100 g	Filo pastry

Chocolate and Hazelnut Mousse

100 g	Chocolate
30 g	Hazelnut paste
100 g	Whipping cream

Apple Calvados Sauce

50 g	Sugar
100 mL	Fresh apple juice
1 tsp	Calvados
10 mL	Heavy cream

Apple Chips

1	Apple, thinly sliced
30 g	Icing sugar

Garnish

4 tsp	Icing sugar
2	Vanilla pods, halved lengthwise
100 g	Apple sherbet

PREPARATION AND PRESENTATION

1. Caramelised apples
   Cut the apples into wedges.
   In a saucepan, caramelise the sugar over medium heat, then add the apples and sauté for 6 minutes.
   Remove from the heat and set aside.

2. Sugar crisp
   Preheat the oven to 150°C.
   Combine the clarified butter, sugar and cinnamon powder in a bowl, and mix well.
   Brush a sheet of filo pastry with this mixture, then place another sheet of filo pastry over.
   Smoothen out the creases and brush the second sheet of filo with the mixture. Cover with another filo sheet.
   Repeat this step until there are 4 layers of filo.
   Cut into 8 rectangles measuring 12 by 4 cm each.
   Arrange the rectangles on a baking tray and bake in the oven for 10 minutes until crispy and golden brown.
   Remove from the heat and set aside.

3. Chocolate and hazelnut mousse
   Place the chocolate in a mixing bowl and melt it in a double boiler.
   Add the hazelnut paste and use a plastic spatula to mix well. Remove from the heat and set aside to rest.
   Whip the cream until light and fluffy, then gently fold it into the chocolate mixture.
   Refrigerate for at least 1 hour before serving.

4. Apple Calvados sauce
   In a saucepan, caramelise the sugar over medium heat, then add the Calvados, apple juice and heavy cream.
   Mix well and cook for a further 5 minutes.
   Process the mixture in the electric blender on high speed until smooth.
   Pass the mixture through a fine sieve and set aside.

5. Apple chips
   Preheat the oven to 80°C.
   Dust the apple slices with icing sugar and bake them in the oven for 2 hours until crispy.
   Remove from the heat and set aside to cool.
   Store in an airtight container until used.

6. To finish and serve
   Layer the sugar crisps and apples on 4 plates as shown, dusting the top layer of sugar crisp with icing sugar.
   Spoon some chocolate mousse on the side and garnish with the apple chips and half a vanilla pod.
   Serve with some apple Calvados sauce and a scoop of apple sherbet on the side.

Chef's Notes
– Peaches, pears and mangoes may also be used in this recipe. But the cooking time has to be adjusted accordingly.
– Apple sherbet may be substituted with your preferred flavour of sherbet or ice cream.
– The sweetness and concentration of tropical fruit flavours in the Semillon Blanc set off the apple's acidity perfectly.

Apple Composition.

Chapter Two

THE TIFFIN ROOM

The tiffin tradition is amongst Raffles' oldest. It started back in 1892 when Tigran Sarkies, the earnest Armenian hotelkeeper who founded Raffles a few years earlier, opened Raffles Tiffin Rooms in the heart of Singapore's business district so that hotel residents had the convenience of dining in town. The venture was an immediate success and it wasn't long before Mr Sarkies was improving and extending the premises. Tiffin, then defined as a light mid-day meal, was served promptly at one o'clock.

Since then, tiffin has remained an integral part of Raffles' fare. For most of this century a mild chicken curry was one of the few Asian mainstays on the hotel's daily menu, while the partaking of Sunday tiffin was an essential aspect of colonial life. This was a substantial meal consisting of mulligatawny followed by a selection of curries, western dishes such as oxtail stew and potato salad, and a multitude of sambals and chutneys all washed down with beer.

Today, Raffles' tiffin buffet can be enjoyed for lunch or dinner. The buffet style enables the adventurous to sample a little of everything, while the more cautious can make a selection to suit their tastes and dietary habits. It also echoes the traditional Asian home-style dining habit of sharing several dishes at any one meal. Presiding over the food is Yogesh Arora, an Indian chef whose association with Raffles dates back to 1996. His boss, Head Caterer Tan Meng Jin, was none other than the maternal grandfather of Raffles International Limited's Chief Operating Officer Jennie Chua.

The buffet has been updated to suit tastebuds discerning and diverse. Immediately noticeable is the emphasis on regional flavours. Indian curries, such as the butter chicken and Madras fish curry, Indonesian favourites, such as gado gado and rojak, and Malay dishes, including beef serunding and acar kuning, take pride of place on the buffet table alongside the traditional mulligatawny soup, oxtail and chicken curry.

The Tiffin Room is one of Raffles' busiest restaurants, also serving breakfast and high tea buffets. Indeed, many would agree that a meal in the Tiffin Room has become one of the rites of passage of world travellers — alongside imbibing a Singapore Sling at the Long Bar.

Twice a day, for lunch and dinner, Tiffin Room staff prepare the sumptuous tiffin buffet spread.

APPETIZERS

ℬEEF SERUNDING

Serves 4

350 g	Beef tenderloin, sliced ¹/₂-cm thick
1 tsp	Coriander powder
1 tsp	Turmeric powder
1 tsp	Salt

Marinate the beef with these ingredients and chill for 2 hours

Serunding

100 g	Freshly grated coconut
1 stalk	Lemon grass, finely chopped
1 tbsp	Blue ginger, finely chopped
1 tbsp	Young ginger, finely chopped
1	Garlic clove, finely chopped
¹/₂ tsp	Chilli paste
¹/₂ tsp	Turmeric powder
10 g	Shallots, peeled and finely chopped
¹/₂	Lime leaf
¹/₂ tsp	Salt
1 tsp	Sugar
4 tbsp	Vegetable oil

Sauce

70 g	Sugar
150 mL	Coconut milk
¹/₄ tsp	Salt
¹/₂ tsp	Chilli paste
10 tbsp	Vegetable oil

PREPARATION AND PRESENTATION

1. Serunding
   Heat the vegetable oil in a wok or frying pan, add the shallots, ginger, garlic, lemon grass and blue ginger. Stir-fry on medium heat until light brown. Add the chilli paste and lime leaf, and stir-fry for 2 minutes. Add the grated coconut, turmeric powder and sugar. Stir-fry until the sugar dissolves (2 - 3 minutes). Remove from the heat and set aside.

2. Beef and sauce
   Heat the vegetable oil in a wok or frying pan. Stir-fry the beef until almost done (about 2 minutes). Remove from the heat and set aside.
   Melt the sugar in a frying pan until it turns light brown (caramelized). Add the coconut milk and stir, then add the beef and half the serunding, mixing thoroughly. Remove from the heat.
   Garnish with the remaining serunding.

Chef's Notes
- This dish can be served as an appetizer or side dish.
- Freshly grated coconut may be substituted with desiccated coconut.
- This dish is enjoyed best when served at room temperature.

𝓜ULLIGATAWNY SOUP

A traditional Indian curry-flavoured chicken soup.

Serves 10

1 kg	Chicken bones, coarsely chopped
16 tbsp	Vegetable oil

8	Cloves	
4	Green cardamom pods	
4	Black cardamom pods	A
2	Cassia leaves	
1	Cinnamon stick	

100 g	Red onions	B
35 g	Ginger	Blend with
30 g	Lemon grass	50 mL
20 g	Blue ginger	of water

2	Green chillies, seeded	C
1 tbsp	Cumin seeds	Blend with
1 tbsp	Plain yoghurt	50 mL
25 g	Cashew nuts	of water

¹/₂ tbsp	Turmeric powder	
1 tbsp	Curry powder	D
1 tbsp	Coriander powder	

3 L	Lukewarm water	
1 tbsp	Oatmeal	
25 g	Shallots, fried	
1 tsp	Lemon juice	E
2 tbsp	Black pepper, freshly ground	
	Salt (to taste)	

Garnish

200 g	White rice, cooked
250 g	Chicken breast, boneless
40 g	Shallots, fried
3 tbsp	Chinese parsley, coarsely chopped
1	Lemon, cut into wedges

Mulligatawny Soup.

PREPARATION AND PRESENTATION

Heat the vegetable oil in a cooking pot and add ingredients A. Cook on medium heat for 2 minutes or until lightly browned. Add ingredients B and continue cooking for another 2 minutes. Add the chicken bones and ingredients C and D. Cook over medium heat for 5 minutes, stirring constantly to prevent sticking or burning. Add ingredients E and bring to a boil.
Reduce the heat to medium, add the chicken breast and cook for 20 minutes. Remove the chicken and cut into small cubes. Set aside.
Continue to cook on medium heat for 3 hours. Strain through a medium sieve and season to taste.
To serve, place the rice and cubed chicken pieces in a soup bowl and add the soup.
Garnish with the spring onions, Chinese parsley and fried shallots, with lemon wedges on the side.

Chef's Note
– The origin of this dish dates back to the days of British rule in India in the early 19th century.

$\mathcal{L}$ASAN MACHI
(BANGALORE FRIED GARLIC FISH)

Serves 4

500 g	Red snapper fillets, cut into 1-cm by 4-cm pieces
12	Curry leaves
50 g	Garlic cloves, peeled
1 ½ tbsp	Chilli paste
60 mL	Coconut milk
½ tsp	Salt (for marinating)
½ tsp	Sugar
1 tsp	Coriander powder
1 tsp	Turmeric powder
500 mL	Vegetable oil
½ tsp	Salt (to taste)

PREPARATION AND PRESENTATION

Season the fish with salt, and coriander and turmeric powder. Set aside for 20 minutes.
Add all but 4 tbsp of the oil to a frying pan and deep-fry the fish until it turns golden brown (about 5 minutes). Remove and set aside.

Add 4 tbsp of the remaining oil to a wok (or pan) and fry the garlic until dark brown (about 5 minutes).
Add the curry leaves and fry for about 10 seconds.
Add the chilli paste, sugar and salt.
Cook for 2 minutes before adding the coconut milk and fried fish. Cook for a further 2 minutes (until the paste is dry), then remove from the heat and serve.

Chef's Note
– Best enjoyed at room temperature.

$\mathcal{T}$AHU SUMBAT
(STUFFED SOYA BEAN CAKES WITH SPICY PEANUT SAUCE)

A popular 'hawker' dish on the streets of old Singapore

Serves 4

4	Tahu (soyabean cakes or tofu)
50 g	Bean sprouts, boiled and strained
50 g	Cucumber, julienned
2	Salad or lettuce leaves, cut into 8 pieces
500 mL	Vegetable oil

Peanut sauce

200 g	Roasted peanuts, skinned and finely chopped
2	Fresh red chillies, pounded
2	Garlic cloves, pounded
2 tbsp	Sugar
1 ½ tbsp	Vinegar
150 mL	Tamarind juice
	Salt (to taste)

PREPARATION AND PRESENTATION

Mix all the ingredients of the peanut sauce dressing thoroughly in a bowl and set aside.
Heat the vegetable oil in a wok and deep-fry the tahu until golden brown. Remove and set aside to cool.
When the tahu has cooled, cut it in half diagonally. Slit the white side and fill the tahu with salad leaf pieces, cucumber and bean sprouts.
Pour the peanut sauce dressing over the stuffed tahu and serve immediately.

ALOO CHAT
(INDIAN POTATO SALAD)

An easily prepared dish, popular with the first wave of Indian immigrants to Singapore.

Serves 4

200 g	Boiled potatoes, peeled and cut into 1-cm cubes
1/2 tsp	Salt
1/2 tsp	Chat masala or lemon juice
1/2 tsp	Cumin seeds, roasted and crushed
1/2 tsp	Coriander seeds, roasted and crushed
3/4 tsp	Chilli powder
2 stalks	Chinese parsley leaves, chopped

PREPARATION AND PRESENTATION
Place the potatoes in a bowl and sprinkle with the salt, cumin, coriander seed, chilli powder and chat masala. Mix thoroughly, add the Chinese parsley leaves. Allow to marinate for 1 hour before serving.

PIAZ SALAT
(INDIAN ONION SALAD)

Serves 4

140 g	Medium red onions, finely sliced
1	Green chilli, finely chopped
3 stalks	Chinese parsley leaves, chopped
1 tsp	Cumin seeds, roasted and crushed
1 tsp	Salt
1 tsp	Lemon juice
1/2 tsp	Chat masala

PREPARATION AND PRESENTATION
Place the sliced onion in a bowl, add 1/2 tsp salt and let stand for 3 minutes. Rinse thoroughly and squeeze to remove excess liquid.
Place the onion, 1/2 tsp salt, green chilli, cumin seed, lemon juice, chat masala and Chinese parsley leaves in a serving bowl. Mix thoroughly and serve.

MAIN DISHES

KAYSARI CHAWAL
(NORTHERN INDIAN SAFFRON RICE)

Serves 6

500 g	Basmati rice
120 mL	Evaporated milk
500 mL	Water
150 g	Ghee
1 pinch	Saffron threads (soak in 3 tbsp of warm water)
1 1/2 tsp	Salt (to taste)
1/2 tsp	Turmeric powder
50 g	Sliced shallots, fried (for garnish)

50 g	Medium red onions, sliced	
1	Cinnamon stick	
8	Cloves	
8	Green cardamom pods	A
3	Cassia or cinnamon leaves	
6	Black cardamom pods	

PREPARATION AND PRESENTATION
Wash the rice and allow to soak in water for 5 minutes, then drain. Melt the ghee in a medium cooking pot over low heat. Add ingredients A and fry until fragrant and light brown (2 - 3 minutes).
Add the turmeric, salt and rice, and cook for 1 minute. Pour in the water and evaporated milk, mix well and bring to a boil. Lower the heat to medium and cook until all the liquid has been absorbed, stirring only once (or the rice will break up and become starchy).
Add the saffron and cover (do not stir). Cook on a very low heat for about 15 minutes, then turn off the heat and leave the cover on for another 15 minutes.
Remove the dry spices and serve, garnished with the fried shallots.
Best served with curries and chutneys.

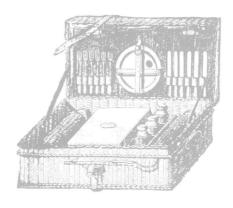

PEA PILAU

A well known and popular northern Indian rice dish

Serves 6

500 g	Basmati rice
120 mL	Evaporated milk
600 mL	Water
1	Medium onion, thinly sliced
120 g	Ghee
1 tsp	Cumin seeds
1 1/2 tsp	Salt
1/2 tsp	Turmeric powder
150 g	Green peas
50 g	Sliced shallots, fried (for garnish)

1	Cinnamon stick	
8	Whole cloves	
8	Green cardamom pods	} A
3	Cassia or cinnamon leaves	
4	Black cardamom pods	

PREPARATION AND PRESENTATION

Wash the rice and allow it to soak in water for
5 minutes. Drain and set aside.
Melt the ghee in a medium cooking pot over low heat,
add ingredients A and fry to release their fragrance
(2 - 3 minutes).
Add the cumin seeds and onions and cook for about
2 minutes or until the onions are lightly browned.
Next, add the turmeric, salt and rice. Stir-fry for
1 minute. Add the water and milk, and bring to a boil
over high heat.
Lower the heat to medium and continue cooking until
all the liquid has been absorbed, stirring only once
(or the rice will break up and become starchy).
Add the green peas and cover. Reduce the heat to
low. Cook for about 15 minutes, turn off the heat,
but do not remove the cover for a further 10 minutes.
Remove the dry spices. Garnish with the fried shallots
and serve.

BOMBAY EGG KURMA

A spicy northern Indian curry dish with eggs

Serves 4

8	Hard-boiled eggs, peeled and deep-fried
3	Medium red onions (slice 1 finely and blend the rest to a fine purée)
40 g	Ginger, finely blended
30 g	Garlic, finely blended
150 g	Medium tomatoes, blended to a purée
1	Cinnamon stick (3-cm)
8	Cloves
8	Green cardamom pods
2	Cinnamon leaves

1 1/2 tbsp	Meat curry powder	Mix in a bowl with 50 mL
1/4 tbsp	Turmeric powder	of water, working into
1/2 tbsp	Coriander powder	a paste

2	Green chillies, cut in half lengthwise
2	Medium tomatoes, cut in half
3 stalks	Chinese parsley leaves, chopped
10 g	Raw cashew nuts, finely pounded
1/2 tbsp	Salt
8 tbsp	Vegetable oil
100 mL	Evaporated milk
1/2 tsp	Green cardamom powder
200 mL	Water

PREPARATION AND PRESENTATION

Heat the vegetable oil in a pan, add the cinnamon stick,
cloves, green cardamom pods, cinnamon leaves and
sliced onions. Fry over medium heat until onions are
soft (2 - 3 minutes).
Add the blended onions, ginger and garlic. Fry over
low heat until light brown (about 2 minutes).
Add tomato purée and curry paste, and cook for
10 minutes over low heat.
Add the water and cook for 1 minute, stirring
continuously to prevent the mixture from sticking to
the pan.
Add the pounded cashew nuts, salt, green chillies and
tomatoes. Cook for 5 minutes, then add the fried eggs,
evaporated milk, cardamom powder, Chinese parsley
leaves and salt. Stir, remove from the heat and serve.

*Clockwise from top: Piaz Salat, Aloo Chat, Tahu Sumbat and
Beef Serunding.*

Calcutta sabzi
(INDIAN VEGETABLE CURRY)

Serves 4

110 g	Medium red onions, finely sliced
30 g	Ginger, finely blended
30 g	Garlic, finely blended
2	Medium tomatoes, blended
1	Cinnamon stick
6	Cloves
1/2 tbsp	Cumin seeds, roasted in a pan and crushed
1/2 tbsp	Black pepper, crushed
1/4 tbsp	Chilli powder
1/2 tbsp	Turmeric powder
1/2 tbsp	Coriander powder
1 tbsp	Meat curry powder
100 g	Carrots, peeled and cut into 1-cm by 3-cm pieces
100 g	Potatoes, peeled and cut into 3-cm cubes
120 g	Cauliflower, divided into florets
100 g	French beans, cut into 3-cm pieces
4 stalks	Chinese parsley leaves, chopped
8 tbsp	Vegetable oil
1/2 tbsp	Tomato paste
400 mL	Water
	Salt (to taste)

PREPARATION AND PRESENTATION

Heat the vegetable oil in a pan, add the cinnamon stick, cloves, cumin seeds, black pepper and onions and stir-fry for 2 minutes over low heat. Add the blended ginger and garlic and stir-fry for 2 minutes. Then add the blended tomatoes and cook for a further 5 minutes.

Add the coriander powder, meat curry powder, turmeric and chilli powder, and cook for 3 minutes. Add the water and tomato paste, and season to taste. Bring the mixture to a boil. Add the carrots, potatoes, cauliflower and French beans. Cover and cook until the vegetables are done (about 15 minutes), then serve.

Oxtail curry

Serves 4

1 kg	Oxtail, cut into medium sized cubes

50 g	Shallots	
10 g	Ginger	
25 g	Garlic	Mix with
1 stalk	Lemon grass	200 mL
6 g	Blue ginger	of water
4	Candlenuts	and blend
1/2 tsp	Dried shrimp paste	to a
3	Lime leaves	fine paste
45 g	Fresh red chillies	
50 g	Fresh yellow ginger	
16 tbsp	Vegetable oil	

75 mL	Tamarind juice	
2 tbsp	Tomato paste	
1/2 tbsp	Sugar	A
2 tsp	Salt (to taste)	
50 g	Chilli paste	
750 mL	Water	

PREPARATION AND PRESENTATION

Heat 8 tbsp of oil in a large pot. Stir-fry the oxtail cubes over medium heat until they turn golden brown (about 15 minutes).

Heat the remaining vegetable oil in a separate large pot. Add the blended paste and stir-fry for about 15 minutes over medium heat. Add the oxtail cubes and ingredients A. Mix well.

Cover and cook on medium heat for 2 hours or until the meat is tender, stirring from time to time to prevent the contents sticking to the pot. Also ensure that the mixture does not dry out — add more water if necessary. Season to taste and serve with rice.

ℳADRAS FISH CURRY

Serves 4

600 g	Red snapper fillet (boneless and skinless), cut to 3-cm cubes
2	Medium red onions, sliced
10 g	Ginger, finely chopped
4	Garlic cloves, finely chopped
1 sprig	Curry leaves
1 tsp	Mustard seeds
1 tsp	Fenugreek seeds
75 mL	Tamarind juice
4 tbsp	Fish curry powder, mixed with 75 mL of water to form a paste
6	Ladies fingers (small), ends cut off
2	Green chillies (with seeds), cut in half lengthwise
2	Red chillies (with seeds), cut in half lengthwise
120 g	Fresh tomatoes, cut in half
80 g	Eggplant, cut into 6 equal pieces
300 mL	Water
8 tbsp	Vegetable oil
2 tsp	Salt

PREPARATION AND PRESENTATION

Heat the vegetable oil in a pan. Stir-fry the ladies fingers and eggplant over medium heat for 1 minute. Remove from the pan and set aside.

In the same pan, brown the mustard and fenugreek seeds over low heat for about 2 minutes. Add the curry leaves and onions and stir-fry until soft. Then add the ginger and garlic and stir-fry for a further 2 minutes.

Add the fish curry paste and cook until the oil separates. Then add the tamarind, salt and water, bring to a boil and cook for about 2 minutes.

Lastly, add the fish, tomatoes, red and green chillies, ladies fingers and eggplant. Cover and simmer for 10 minutes. Remove from the heat.

Serve with white rice, mango chutney and papadam.

𝒮AMBAL PRAWNS
(SPICY CHILLI PRAWNS)

A traditional Malay dish served as an accompaniment

Serves 4

60 g	Medium red onions, blended	
20 g	Ginger, blended	A
30 g	Garlic, blended	
2 stalks	Lemon grass, crushed	
1 tsp	Blue ginger, blended	
300 g	Chilli paste	
1/2 tbsp	Dried shrimp, finely pounded	
1 tbsp	Tomato paste	
75 mL	Tamarind juice	
120 g	Medium tomatoes, cut into quarters	
1/2 tbsp	Sugar	
1 tsp	Salt (to taste)	
8 tbsp	Vegetable oil	
16	Medium-large prawns (de-shelled and de-veined), tail on	
1/2 tbsp	Shrimp paste	

PREPARATION AND PRESENTATION

Heat the vegetable oil in a pot, add ingredients A and stir-fry over medium heat for about 2 minutes. Do not allow to brown.

Add the chilli paste, dried shrimp paste and dried shrimp, and stir-fry over low heat for 10 minutes. Add the tomato paste, sugar, tamarind juice and salt, and stir constantly for another 5 minutes.

Add the prawns and tomatoes. Cook over medium heat until the prawns are done (5 - 8 minutes).

Serve with rice.

Chef's Note
– The prawns can also be cooked whole, in their shells.

Following pages: Madras Fish Curry, Kaisari Chawal, Hyderabadi Sag Gosh and Sambal Prawns.

$\mathcal{M}$URGH MAKHANI
(BUTTER CHICKEN)

Serves 4

1	Whole chicken (2 - 2.5 kg), skin removed, deboned, cut into bite-sized pieces

5 tbsp	Vegetable oil
1 tsp	Cumin seeds, crushed
30 g	Garlic, finely chopped
30 g	Onion, finely chopped
200 g	Fresh tomatoes, blended
300 mL	Evaporated milk
$^1/_2$ tsp	Cardamom powder

150 g	Unsalted butter	
2 tbsp	Tomato paste	
1 tbsp	Meat curry powder	
1 tsp	White pepper powder	A
$^3/_4$ tsp	Sugar	
$^3/_4$ tsp	Salt	
250 mL	Water	

Marinade

200 g	Plain yoghurt
$^1/_2$ tbsp	Ginger, finely blended
$^1/_2$ tbsp	Garlic, finely blended
1 tbsp	Tomato ketchup
$^1/_2$ tbsp	Lime juice
$^1/_4$ tbsp	White pepper
$^1/_2$ tbsp	Coriander powder
$^1/_2$ tbsp	Cumin powder
$^1/_2$ tbsp	Chilli powder
$^1/_4$ tsp	Egg-yellow food colouring
1 tsp	Salt (to taste)

PREPARATION AND PRESENTATION

1. Marinating the chicken
   Combine all marinade ingredients and add the chicken. Set aside for about 8 hours or overnight.
   Preheat the oven to 230°C.
   Place the marinated chicken on a baking tray and roast in the oven for 20 minutes.
2. Finishing
   Heat the vegetable oil in a frying pan or wok. Add the cumin seeds, onion and garlic, and brown over medium heat for about 2 minutes. Add the blended tomatoes and cook for 10 minutes.
   Add ingredients A and allow to boil for 5 minutes.
   Add the marinated chicken and cook on medium heat for 10 minutes. Add the evaporated milk, stir and remove from the heat.
   Before serving, add the cardamom powder and stir.

$\mathcal{H}$YDERABADI SAG GOSHT
(LAMB IN SPINACH)

Serves 4

400 g	Lamb leg, boneless, cut into 4-cm cubes
250 g	Spinach, washed and cut into small pieces
$^1/_2$ tsp	White pepper
1 tsp	Salt
5 tbsp	Evaporated milk
100 g	Unsalted butter
2 tbsp	Plain yoghurt
250 mL	Water
8 tbsp	Vegetable oil

$^1/_2$ tbsp	Coriander powder	
$^1/_2$ tbsp	Cumin powder	A
2 tbsp	Turmeric powder	
2 tbsp	Meat curry powder	

2	Cinnamon sticks	
8	Cloves	
30 g	Onions, chopped	
20 g	Ginger, chopped	B
20 g	Garlic, chopped	
1	Large tomato, chopped	
8 g	Fenugreek leaves	
2	Green chillies, sliced	

1 tbsp	Sliced shallots, fried	
1 tbsp	Chinese parsley	Garnish
4 tbsp	Fresh cream	

PREPARATION AND PRESENTATION

Boil the spinach in water for 3 minutes, drain and blend finely with 500 mL of water.
Marinate the lamb with the salt and ingredients A. Set aside for 2 - 3 hours.
Heat the vegetable oil in a pot. Add ingredients B and stir-fry for 2 minutes.
Add the ginger and garlic, and stir-fry until light brown (about 2 minutes). Then add the tomato and cook for another 3 minutes. Add the seasoned lamb and cook on medium heat for 5 minutes.
Next, add the yoghurt, white pepper and water. Cover and cook on low heat until the meat is tender (about $^1/_2$ hour).
Add the blended spinach and cook for 5 minutes, then add the cream and butter. Stir well and remove from the heat.
To serve, garnish with chopped Chinese parsley, fried shallots and 1 tbsp of fresh cream.

Clockwise from top: Pea Pilau, Calcutta Shabj, Murgh Makhani, Bombay Egg Kurma and Oxtail Curry.

CONDIMENTS

ACAR KUNING

Serves 4

1 stalk	Lemon grass (fresh), crushed
4 tbsp	Vegetable oil
1 tbsp	Chilli paste
1/2 tsp	Turmeric powder
100 mL	Vinegar
1 tbsp	Sugar
2 tsp	Salt
300 mL	Water

Onion Paste

1	Onion	Add 50 mL
10 g	Ginger	of water and
15 g	Garlic	blend finely
6 g	Candlenuts	to a paste

Vegetables

100 g	Cucumbers, seeded and cut into 1-cm by 3-cm pieces
60 g	Carrots, cut into 1/2-cm by 3-cm pieces
8	Garlic cloves, cut in half lengthwise and skin removed
30 g	Ginger, cut into 1-cm by 3½-cm strips and skin removed
1	Fresh red chilli, seeds removed, 1-cm by 3-cm strips
4	Small whole shallots, peeled

PREPARATION AND PRESENTATION

Soak the vegetables in a pot of water with 2 tbsp of salt for 15 minutes, rinse under running water and drain.

Heat the vegetable oil in a small pot. Add lemon grass and the blended onion paste. Cook over low heat for 5 - 7 minutes.

Add the turmeric powder, 1/2 tsp salt, sugar and vinegar, and cook for 2 minutes. Then add the seasoned vegetables. Stir well.

Remove the vegetables from the heat, allow to cool and place in a serving container.

Chef's Notes
- This dish may be served hot or cold with curry and rice.
- It can be kept chilled for 2 weeks.

PINEAPPLE ACAR

A traditional Nonya appetizer with a tangy, sweet-and-sour flavour

Serves 4

1	Young pineapple, skin removed, cored and cut into 2-cm by 3-cm cubes
100 g	Red sugar
1 tsp	Salt
1	Cinnamon stick
2	Cloves
3	Green cardamom pods
1/2	Red onion, thickly sliced
1/2	Fresh red chilli, seeded, cut into thin strips
2 tbsp	Vegetable oil
1/2 tsp	Turmeric powder
1 L	Water

PREPARATION AND PRESENTATION

Bring the water to a boil in a large pot. Add the salt, turmeric and pineapple cubes. Continue to boil for 2 minutes. Strain and set aside.

Heat the vegetable oil in a frying pan over medium heat. Add the cloves, cardamom, cinnamon and onion. Fry until the onions are soft, then add the red chilli, seasoned pineapple cubes and red sugar. Stir.

Simmer for 2 minutes on low heat, remove and set aside to cool. Remove the spices before serving but do not drain the liquid.

Chef's Notes
- Pineapple Acar can be kept chilled for up to 2 weeks.
- This dish can be served to accompany most curry dishes.

Clockwise from top right: Pineapple Acar, Pickled Shallots, Mango Chutney, Lime Pickles, Mint Chutney, Acar Kuning, Vegetable Acar and Mixed Pickles.

VEGETABLE ACAR

Serves 4

90 g	Cucumbers, seeded and cut to 1-cm by 3$^{1}/_{2}$-cm strips
90 g	Carrots, cut to $^{1}/_{2}$-cm by 3$^{1}/_{2}$-cm pieces
10 g	Young ginger, skinned and cut to 1-cm by 3$^{1}/_{2}$-cm pieces
10 g	Garlic cloves, cut in half lengthwise
1	Red chilli, seeds removed, cut in half and quartered lengthwise
4	Small shallots, peeled
200 mL	Vinegar
2 tbsp	Sugar
100 mL	Water
$^{1}/_{2}$ tbsp	Salt

PREPARATION AND PRESENTATION

Place the water, sugar, salt and vinegar in a bowl. Stir to dissolve the sugar and salt.
Add all the vegetables and marinate for at least 8 hours. Drain before serving. May be served with all curries.

Chef's Note
– This dish can be kept chilled for up to 1 week.

LIME PICKLES

Yields about 1.5 kg

25	Whole limes (3 - 4-cm in diameter)
400 g	Salt
200 g	Green chillies, cut lengthwise into 3-cm strips
35 g	Cumin seed, pounded
50 g	Mustard seed, roasted and skinned
300 mL	Indian sesame oil
300 mL	Vinegar
90 g	Garlic cloves, thickly sliced
60 g	Young ginger, cut into 1-cm slices

PREPARATION AND PRESENTATION

1. Preparing the limes for pickling
Wash and dry the limes. Spread a layer of salt about 2.5-cm deep in the bottom of a large plastic container. Place the limes on the salt and alternate limes and salt until the container is filled. Set aside for 2 - 3 weeks at room temperature.

2. Pickling the limes
Cut the salted limes into quarters. Thoroughly mix the sesame oil, vinegar, garlic, ginger, chillies, cumin seeds and mustard seeds, then pour the mixture over the salted limes.
Put the salted limes and the pickling mixture into a clean glass container. Set aside for about 2 weeks at room temperature before using.

PERDESI AM CHUTNEY
(MANGO CHUTNEY)

Yields about 1.25 kg

1.25 kg	Mangoes, firm and green, beginning to turn yellow
$^{1}/_{2}$ tbsp	Salt
10 g	Young ginger, chopped
10 g	Onion, chopped
5	Whole, small garlic cloves
20 g	Raisins
10 g	Preserved ginger
300 g	Brown sugar
600 mL	Rice vinegar
6	Red chillies, roughly chopped
15 g	Almonds, shredded and blanched in hot water

1 pinch	Nutmeg powder	
6	Cloves,	} A
10	Whole allspice	

PREPARATION AND PRESENTATION

Peel and cut the mangoes into coarse pieces, sprinkle with salt and allow to stand overnight, refrigerated.
Rinse the mangoes under running water.
Place spices A in a muslin cloth. Tie into a small bag.
In a pot, boil the sugar, vinegar and spice bag for 20 minutes on low heat.
Add the onions, fresh ginger, garlic, raisins and pepper. Boil for a further 10 minutes.
Add half the mangoes and boil for another 15 minutes. Then add the almonds and the remainder of the mangoes and boil for 1 hour, stirring frequently.
Remove and discard the spice bag and set the chutney aside to cool.

Chef's Note
– This dish can be kept chilled for about 1 month.

Clockwise from top: Kueh Lapis Agar-agar, Seri Kaya, Ondeh Ondeh, Bubor Terigu, Pulut Hitam and Takos.

DESSERTS

ℬUBUR TERIGU
(MALAYSIAN WHITE WHEAT PORRIDGE)

Serves 6

150 g	White wheat, washed (terigu or biji gandum)
20 g	Palm sugar, dissolved in 75 mL of water
2 L	Water
3	Pandan leaves, knotted
1/4 tsp	Salt
300 mL	Coconut milk, preferably fresh
5 tbsp	Sugar

PREPARATION AND PRESENTATION

Place the water and pandan leaves in large pot and bring to a boil. Add the white wheat and simmer on low heat until the wheat expands (about 1 hour). Stir occasionally.

Add the sugar, salt and palm sugar. Boil until the sugar dissolves, then add the coconut milk and remove from the heat. Leave to rest for about 15 minutes to allow the wheat to expand further.

Remove the pandan leaves before serving.

Chef's Notes
- This dish may be served hot or cold.
- If fresh pandan leaves are unavailable, a few drops of pandan essence may be used.
- Both Bubur Terigu and Pulut Hitam have their origins in the Malay Peninsula and are a standard staple at home or in restaurants. Simple yet delightful, these desserts may be enjoyed on their own.

𝒫ULUT HITAM
(BLACK GLUTINOUS RICE PUDDING)

Serves 6

100 g	Black glutinous rice
2.5 L	Water
3 tbsp	Sugar
300 mL	Coconut milk, preferably fresh
3 stalks	Pandan leaves, knotted
1/4 tsp	Salt

PREPARATION AND PRESENTATION

Place the water and pandan leaves in a large pot. Bring to a boil, add the glutinous rice and simmer on low heat until the rice is cooked (about 1/2 hour). Stir occasionally.

Add the sugar and salt, then stir. Continue to simmer over medium heat.

Remove from the heat and add the coconut milk, stirring well. Discard pandan leaf. Enjoyed best when served hot.

Chef's Notes
- If the consistency appears too thick, add a little water.
- With most black rice varieties, the cooking time may vary considerably. This, however, should not affect the taste.

𝒪NDEH ONDEH
(SWEET POTATO DUMPLINGS WITH PALM SUGAR, COATED IN COCONUT)

Yields about 50

600 g	Sweet potatoes, peeled
225 g	Glutinous rice flour
100 mL	Warm water
50 mL	Pandan juice (extracted from 9 pandan leaves, pounded or blended with 100 mL of water and strained thoroughly with muslin cloth)
200 g	Palm sugar, finely chopped
300 g	Freshly grated coconut ⎫ Mix together
1 pinch	Salt ⎭ for the coating

PREPARATION AND PRESENTATION

Steam the sweet potatoes for 20 minutes or until soft. While the sweet potatoes are still warm, mash them with a fork and add the flour, warm water and pandan juice. Knead well to a soft dough. Roll the dough into about 50 small balls, 4-cm in diameter.

Make a well in each dumpling and add 1 tbsp of the palm sugar. Reseal the well. Ensure that the dough is not too thick and is well sealed. Coat with additional flour if it is too moist or difficult to roll.

Repeat the process until all dumplings are filled.

Boil the water in a medium-sized pot, then reduce the heat to low. Place the dumplings in the water (they will sink to the bottom). When cooked, the dumplings will rise to the surface (5 - 7 minutes).

Remove the dumplings from the hot water and allow to cool. Coat with the grated coconut before serving.

Chef's Note
- As a dessert, two to three dumplings per serving is ample.
- Biting into the dumpling is an unforgettable taste experience as the liquified palm sugar spouts into your mouth.

*A*BUK ABUK SAGO
(SAGO PEARLS WITH COCONUT AND PALM SUGAR IN A BANANA LEAF)

Yields about 35

250 g	Sago pearls, soaked in water for about 1 hour
125 g	Palm sugar, coarsely chopped
150 mL	Coconut milk, preferably fresh
Pinch	Salt
35	Toothpicks
35	8-cm squares of banana leaves (before cutting, soften the banana leaves by blanching in hot water)

PREPARATION AND PRESENTATION

Drain the sago and mix with the palm sugar, coconut milk and salt.

Fold each banana leaf into a cone and fill it with 1 tbsp of the mixture. Fold the top over and seal firmly with a toothpick.

Repeat until all the mixture has been used.

Place the banana leaves in a steamer for 25 – 35 minutes. Remove and allow to cool before serving.

Chef's Note
- This dessert should be prepared and served on the same day and not kept overnight.

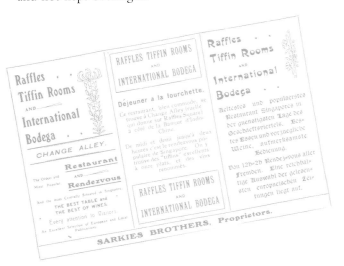

*S*ERI KAYA
(GLUTINOUS RICE STEAMED WITH KAYA CUSTARD)

Special equipment: A round cake tin, 22-cm diameter and 5 - 7-cm height

Yields about 1.5 kg

300 g	Glutinous rice, soaked in water for 1 hour
200 mL	Coconut milk
1/2 tsp	Salt
1	Pandan leaf, knotted

Kaya Topping

5	Eggs
500 mL	Coconut milk
30 g	Glutinous rice flour
120 g	Sugar
20 mL	Pandan juice (extracted from 5 pandan leaves, pounded or blended with 50 mL of water and strained thoroughly with muslin cloth)
Pinch	Salt

PREPARATION AND PRESENTATION

1. Rice

   Drain the rice. In a large pot, mix the rice, salt, pandan leaves and the 200 mL of coconut milk. Spoon the mixture into the cake tin. Steam until cooked (about 1/2 hour), then remove the knotted pandan leaf. Even out the top layer with a spatula.

2. Kaya topping

   Lightly beat the eggs and sugar. Add the rice flour, salt, pandan juice and 500 mL of coconut milk. Stir, then sieve the mixture and pour it evenly over the rice. Steam for another 1/2 hour or until set. Remove from the heat and allow to cool before serving.

3. To serve

   Slice into desired sizes. Rice will have a sticky but firm consistency. Do not stack the slices. Keep in a cool, dry place before serving.

Chef's Note
- This recipe can also be prepared with small individual moulds.

Chapter Three

THE EMPIRE CAFE

The Empire Cafe is a casual, cosy cross between a modern hotel coffee house and an old-fashioned *kopi tiam*. Throughout the day it serves a steady stream of hotel residents and downtown office workers, families with children in tow and tourists who take a break from sightseeing to sip a tall, cool drink.

The Singapore-of-yesteryear ambience is created by the marble-topped and tooled teakwood-base tables and bentwood-style chairs reminiscent of the corner coffee shops of old. The nostalgic mood is heightened by the noisy din as the clatter of bowls and glasses competes with the chatter of diners, the sounds reverberating off marble floors and tiled walls. Tables next to the large, lace-curtained windows are especially coveted as they offer a wonderful vantage point for watching the parade of humanity that passes under the covered walkway outside.

The food is eclectic. Although visitors can enjoy such international staples as club sandwiches, omelettes and hamburgers, it is the local dishes that have found a devoted following among residents and visitors alike. These dishes are prepared by a team of highly specialized chefs who pride themselves on preserving Singapore's culinary heritage.

To reinterpret the past, the chefs went back to basics and used their culinary networks to track down old recipes and preparation methods. Many of the cafe's most popular dishes have their roots in hawker food; famous street hawkers were often known for a single dish, perfecting it through years and years of repeated preparation. Recipes in hand, the chefs turned their attention to the presentation of the food. In the days before plastic, hawkers relied heavily on leaves. A helping of Cha Tau Kueh (Carrot Cake), was dished out on an *opeh* leaf, the outer leaf of the palm, and a coconut husk was used as an eating utensil. The same presentation has been successfully adapted at the Empire Cafe. Those who order the Roti Prata and Murtabak will also find their meal served the old-fashioned way, on banana leaves.

Thus, it is not surprising that patrons return time and again to savour the cafe's Hainanese Chicken Rice, Sliced Fish Bee Hoon, Curry Laksa, Roti Prata, Chicken Curry, or even the more exotic Herbal Black Chicken Soup.

Marble-topped tables and bentwood-style chairs at the Empire Cafe are so reminiscent of Singapore's old kopi tiams.

HAINANESE CHICKEN RICE

Serves 4

1	Whole, fresh chicken (boilers), about 2 kg
1	Garlic clove, slightly bruised and crushed
2	Pandan leaves
30 g	Ginger, slightly crushed
4 tbsp	Sesame oil
	Salt (to taste)
	Water (enough to completely immerse the chicken in the pot)
	Tomato and cucumber slices (for chicken garnish)

Chicken Soup Garnish

1 tbsp	Preserved Chinese cabbage (tien tsin)
1 tbsp	Spring onions, sliced
1 tbsp	Sliced shallots, fried

Chicken-flavoured Rice

500 g	Rice
	Chicken fat (removed from the chicken)
20 g	Shallots, sliced
60 g	Ginger, slightly crushed
1	Pandan leaf
1 L	Chicken stock (from cooking the chicken)
1 tbsp	Salt

Ginger Sauce

20 g	Ginger	
5 g	Garlic	
5 tbsp	Chicken stock	} Blend
1/4 tsp	Salt	
1/2 tsp	Sesame oil	

Chilli Sauce

60 g	Chilli	
10 g	Ginger	
10 g	Garlic	
1 tbsp	Chinese rice vinegar	
1/2 tsp	Salt	} Blend
1/2 tsp	Sugar	
1 tsp	Sesame oil	
4 tbsp	Chicken stock	

PREPARATION AND PRESENTATION

1. Chicken
   Remove any excess fat from the chicken (set aside for cooking the rice).
   Add the water, ginger, garlic and pandan leaves to a large pot and bring to a boil. Add the chicken and reduce the heat to low. Make sure the water covers the whole chicken. Poach for approximately 45 minutes. Remove the chicken and cool it under running water for 3 minutes. Keep the chicken stock for later use. Baste the chicken with sesame oil to prevent it from drying out.

2. Chicken soup
   Debone the chicken. Add the bones to the balance of the stock. Bring to a boil and cook for 20 - 25 minutes. Strain and set aside.

3. Chicken-flavoured rice
   Melt the chicken fat in a pot, add the sliced shallots and ginger and lightly sauté for 2 minutes. Remove and discard excess chicken fat solids.
   Wash and drain the rice. Place in a rice cooker with 1 litre of the chicken stock, pandan leaf, sautéed shallots, ginger and 1 tsp salt. Mix well and cook as you would for plain rice.

4. Finishing
   Cut the deboned chicken into serving-size pieces. Place them on a small plate and garnish with the tomato and cucumber slices.
   The soup should be garnished with sliced spring onions, fried shallots and preserved Chinese cabbage.
   Serve with dark soya sauce, ginger sauce, chilli sauce, and the rice. The soup and the rice should ideally be served hot and the chicken, at room temperature.

Chef's Note
- This dish originated on the island of Hainan. It has evolved through the years into a truly classic Singaporean dish.

Sliced Fish Bee Hoon and Hainanese Chicken Rice.

Hong Sau Tofu

A favourite dish among our vegetarian patrons

Serves 4

360 g	Beancurd (fresh, semi-firm), cut into triangles or squares
40 g	Onions, cut into 2-cm cubes
30 g	Ginger, peeled and very thinly sliced
2 tbsp	Light soya sauce
4 tbsp	Vegetarian oyster sauce
2 tsp	Sesame oil
800 mL	Water
2 tbsp	Cornstarch (mixed with 2 tbsp of water)
4 tbsp	Vegetable oil
	Salt and pepper to taste

Vegetables

40 g	Shiitake mushrooms, medium, cut in half
40 g	Carrots, sliced thinly
40 g	Fresh button mushrooms, cut in half
40 g	Straw mushrooms, cut in half
40 g	Green peppers, cut into 2-cm cubes
40 g	Black fungus (pre-soaked), cut in half
160 g	Choy sum

PREPARATION AND PRESENTATION

Deep-fry the beancurd until golden. Drain excess oil with paper towel. Set aside.

Heat a wok, add the oil and sauté the sliced ginger and onions until fragrant (1 minute).

Add all the vegetables. Stir-fry for 1 minute, then add the soya sauce, vegetarian oyster sauce and sesame oil, and fry for another minute.

Add the water, bring to a boil and thicken with the cornstarch mixture. Season to taste.

Transfer to a heated clay pot and serve with steamed rice on the side.

Chef's Notes

- Choy sum is a typical and very popular leafy vegetable. Any other similar leafy greens may be used as a substitute.
- You may personalize this dish by using any vegetables of your choice.

Laksa (THICK RICE NOODLES WITH SEAFOOD IN COCONUT-CURRY GRAVY)

Serves 4 - 6

100 g	Shallots	
20 g	Garlic	
20 g	Dried shrimp paste	
2 stalks	Lemon grass, fresh	
20 g	Candlenuts	A
20 g	Blue ginger, sliced	
20 g	Turmeric	
30 g	Dried shrimps	
12	Dried red chillies	

800 mL	Coconut milk, preferably fresh
800 mL	Water
500 g	Laksa noodles or dried thick rice vermicelli

Garnish

12	Slices of cooked fish cake
12	Slices of deep fried beancurd or tofu
1/2	Cucumber, cut into fine strips
100 g	Beansprouts
12	Fresh prawns, medium, shelled and cooked, tail-on
3	Laksa leaves, 1 chopped, 2 whole
3 tbsp	Cooking oil
	Salt, pepper to taste
1 tsp	Sugar

PREPARATION AND PRESENTATION

Pound ingredients A in a mortar until fine.

Heat the oil in a pot, add the pounded ingredients and fry over low heat until fragrant (4 - 5 minutes). Add the whole laksa leaves.

Add water, bring to a boil and simmer over low heat for 15 minutes. Add the coconut milk and bring the mixture to the boil again. Season to taste, remove from the heat and set aside.

Blanch the beansprouts and noodles in boiling water.

To serve, place equal amounts of noodles in individual serving dishes. Garnish with the deep fried beancurd, cucumber, beansprouts, prawns and fish cake. Pour the gravy into the bowls and sprinkle with the chopped laksa leaf. Serve hot.

Chef's Notes

- You may use any type of thick Oriental rice or egg noodles.
- You may add sambal chilli to make the dish extra spicy.

Hong Sau Tofu (top) and Laksa.

𝒦ARI AYAM
(MALAY CHICKEN CURRY)

Serves 4

1 kg	Fresh chicken, skinned and cut into 12 pieces
4 tbsp	Vegetable oil
4 tbsp	Ghee
1	Cinnamon stick
2	Cardamom seeds
2	Star anise
2	Cloves
1	Pandan leaf
5 g	Garlic, sliced
110 g	Red onions, sliced

} A

1 tbsp	Coriander powder
1 tbsp	Chilli powder
1 tsp	Turmeric powder
1 tsp	Fennel powder
1 tsp	Cumin powder
1 1/2 tbsp	Meat curry powder

} Mix with 40 mL water to form a paste

160 g	Tomatoes, cut into quarters
400 g	Medium potatoes, peeled and cut into quarters
500 mL	Coconut milk, preferably fresh
25 g	Green chillies, cut in half lengthwise
5 g	Ground ginger
40 g	Plain yoghurt
80 g	Tomato paste
750 mL	Water
	Salt and pepper

PREPARATION AND PRESENTATION

Heat the oil in a pot and melt the ghee. Add ingredients A and fry for 5 minutes over medium heat.

Add the ground ginger, yoghurt and tomato paste, and fry over medium heat for another 10 minutes, stirring constantly to prevent the mixture from sticking to the pot. Add the prepared paste and fry for 5 minutes, then add the chicken pieces and mix well. Pour in the water and bring to a boil. Simmer for 10 minutes over medium heat.

Add the coconut milk and potatoes. Cover and cook for a further 15 minutes. Season to taste.

Serve with plain rice or roti prata.

Chef's Note
- A basic curry but one that is full of flavour and has a long history at Raffles Hotel.

𝒴U PIN (SLICED FISH BEE HOON)

Serves 4

4 tbsp	Cooking oil
1 tbsp	Sesame oil
30 g	Ginger, peeled and sliced
4 tbsp	Chinese rice wine (hua tiao jiou)
60 g	Choy sum
5 tbsp	Light soya sauce
2 L	Fish stock
320 g	Tenggiri or Spanish mackerel fillet, sliced
600 g	Thick rice vermicelli, pre-soaked until soft
20 g	Shallots, fried
20 g	Chinese parsley leaves
1/2 tsp	White pepper powder

Fish Stock

1/2	Fish head, preferably big-head carp (song yu), about 1 kg
50 g	Ginger, peeled and sliced
2 L	Water
50 g	Flour

PREPARATION AND PRESENTATION

1. Fish stock (must be prepared in advance)
   Cut the cleaned fish head into 8 pieces. Coat lightly with flour and deep-fry until golden brown. Set aside. Heat the oil in a wok. Stir-fry the ginger briefly and add water, followed by the fish head pieces. Bring to a boil and simmer for 30 minutes. Strain all the ingredients and set the fish stock aside. Season to taste.

2. Fish
   Heat the oil in a wok, add the sliced ginger and stir-fry quickly. Add the fish stock and bring to a boil. Add the rice vermicelli and cook for further 3 minutes.
   Add the Chinese rice wine, sliced tenggiri and choy sum, and season to taste with light soya sauce. Simmer until the fish is done (1 - 2 minutes). Finish with a few drops of sesame oil.
   Pour the mixture into a bowl. Garnish with fried shallots, Chinese parsley leaves and a dash of pepper, and serve.

Chef's Note
- You may also use other types of firm fish fillet.

Vegetable Curry (top) and Chicken Curry served with Briyani and Steamed Rice.

Soto Ayam (Spicy Malay Chicken Soup with Noodles)

Serves 4

1 tbsp	Barley powder	} mixed with
1 tbsp	Dhal powder	water
800 mL	Coconut milk	
500 g	Chicken breast meat, bone in	
1.5 L	Water	
10 tbsp	Vegetable oil	

Garnish

120 g	Beansprouts, blanched
20 g	Sliced shallots, fried
20 g	Chinese parsley, chopped

120 g	Red onions, chopped	
20 g	Garlic, chopped	A
20 g	Green chilli padi, chopped	

10 g	Briyani powder	
5 g	Fennel powder	B
5 g	Coriander powder	

5 g	Blue ginger	
1	Small cinnamon stick (1-cm)	
2	Star anise	C
1/2 tsp	Turmeric powder	
20 g	Lemon grass	

PREPARATION AND PRESENTATION

Add the water and a pinch of salt to a medium-sized pot and bring to a boil. Poach the chicken over medium heat until tender (about 20 minutes). Remove the chicken and keep the stock for soup. Shred the chicken meat into strips for garnish. Set aside.
Heat the oil in a saucepan and fry ingredients A for about 1 minute. Lower the heat, add ingredients B and fry until fragrant (about 2 minutes).
Add ingredients C and fry for a further 2 minutes. Then add the coconut milk and chicken stock and bring to a boil. Reduce the heat and simmer for 20 - 25 minutes. Season to taste.
Add the barley and dhal powder to thicken the chicken soup, then strain it to remove the spices.
To serve, add the shredded chicken, and garnish with the blanched beansprouts and Chinese parsley.

Chef's Note
- Ketupat (rice cubes, see page 106) or egg noodles may also be added.

Kaki Kambing (Indian Lamb Knuckle Soup)

Serves 4

1 kg	Lamb knuckles, cut into 6 - 8-cm pieces
2 L	Water
6 tbsp	Vegetable oil

1 tbsp	Dhal powder
1 tbsp	Barley powder

1 tbsp	Ginger, pounded	
1 tbsp	Garlic, pounded	A
1 tbsp	Coriander powder	mix to
1 tbsp	Turmeric powder	a smooth paste
1/2 tsp	Ground white pepper	
20 mL	Water	

1	Cinnamon stick	
3	Cloves	B
2	Cardamom seeds	
200 g	Red onions, sliced	

Garnish

20 g	Sliced shallots, fried

PREPARATION AND PRESENTATION

Boil the lamb knuckles in water in a large pot for 1 hour or until meat is almost tender. Set aside.
Heat the oil in a pot, add ingredients B and fry over low heat until fragrant (about 3 minutes). Add the sliced red onions and fry until soft, then add ingredients A and fry on low heat until the oil separates from the other ingredients (about 5 minutes).
Pour the mixture into the pot containing the lamb knuckles and simmer over low heat for 15 minutes. Thicken with barley and dhal powder. Season to taste and serve.

The Empire Cafe offers casual dining and is popular with Singaporeans and travellers alike.

Rojak Buahan
(SPICY TROPICAL FRUIT SALAD)

Serves 4

Salad

8	Red water apple (jambu air)
200 g	Ripe, large Sarawak pineapple
200 g	Half-ripe papaya
2	Half-ripe mangoes
1	Ripe guava

Garnish

16	Local lettuce leaves
2 tsp	Toasted sesame seed
4	Wanton skins, sliced into 1/2-cm strips

Sauce

160 g	Sambal rojak (see *Chef's Notes* below)
4 tbsp	Lukewarm water

PREPARATION AND PRESENTATION

1. Salad and garnish
   Peel and cut each fruit separately into cubes of about 1-cm. Set aside.
   Heat the oil in a wok and deep-fry the wanton skins until golden brown. Remove and place on an absorbent paper towel to drain off excess oil. Set aside.
   Arrange 4 lettuce leaves in a circular shape on a plate. Place the diced fruits on the lettuce leaves.
   Garnish with the crispy wanton skins, and sprinkle toasted sesame seeds over the salad.

2. Sauce
   Mix the sambal rojak with lukewarm water until smooth. Pour the sauce over the salad and serve.

Chef's Notes

- To make sambal rojak, combine the following ingredients and mix well:

4 tbsp	Shrimp paste
80 mL	Tamarind juice
1 tbsp	Sugar
1 tbsp	Lime juice
2 tbsp	Sambal chilli

- Any fresh seasonal fruit can be used to suit individual taste.
- Use Hawaiian pineapple if Sarawak pineapple is unavailable.
- The combination of the acidity and firmness of the mango and papaya, the sweetness of the pineapple and guava, and the juiciness of the jambu air makes this an interesting local dish.

Kari Sayoran
(MALAY VEGETABLE CURRY)

Serves 4

120 g	Carrots, peeled and cut in half lengthwise, then sliced into 1/2-cm thick pieces	
100 g	Long beans, cut into 3-cm pieces	
160 g	Eggplant, cut in half lengthwise, then into 1-cm thick pieces	
160 g	Cauliflower, cut into large florets	
300 mL	Water	
11 tbsp	Vegetable oil	
1/4 tsp	Mustard seeds	
1/4 tsp	Fenugreek seeds	
1 sprig	Curry leaves	A
60 g	Red onions, sliced	
10 g	Ground ginger	
10 g	Ground garlic	
1 tsp	Chilli powder	B
1 tbsp	Coriander powder	Mix with
1 tbsp	Turmeric powder	50 mL of water
1 1/2 tbsp	Fish curry powder	to form
1 tbsp	Fennel powder	a paste
70 mL	Tamarind juice	
100 mL	Coconut milk	
1	Tomato, cut into quarters	C
2	Green chillies, sliced	
10 g	Green peas	

PREPARATION AND PRESENTATION

Heat the oil in a medium cooking pot, add ingredients A and fry for 5 minutes. Add paste B and fry over medium heat until fragrant (about 5 minutes).
Then add the carrots, long beans, cauliflower and eggplant, mixing well.
Gradually add the water. Bring to a boil, reduce the heat and cook over medium heat for 10 minutes. Add ingredients C and cook for 10 minutes. Season to taste. Serve with plain rice or roti prata.

Chef's Note

- A side dish, it can be served as a main dish if you increase the proportions accordingly.

Clockwise from top: Kueh Pie-ti, Carrot Cake, Hokkien Poh Piah and Rojak Buahan.

ROTI PRATA
(TRADITIONAL INDIAN PANCAKES)

Yields about 12

1 kg	Plain flour	
Oil or ghee	For greasing and cooking	
30 mL	Condensed or evaporated milk	
20 g	Salt	
30 g	Sugar	
30 g	Unsalted butter	A
1	Egg, lightly beaten	
500 mL	Water	

PREPARATION AND PRESENTATION

Sift the flour into a mixing bowl, add ingredients A and mix well. Flour your hands and knead until a soft dough is formed. Rest the dough for ¹/₂ hour. Repeat the kneading process twice more.

Shape the dough into 12 small balls and rub with oil or ghee to prevent the balls from sticking together. Leave them overnight in a covered container.

When you are ready to make the prata, spread some oil on a smooth working surface, preferably marble. Place a dough-ball on the surface and flatten it with your palm. Flip the dough to make it paper-thin and circular in shape, about 60-cm in diameter (see *Chef's Note*). Add a few drops of oil. Fold the paper-thin dough into a rectangular shape of 18-cm by 20-cm. Sprinkle some oil on a hot plate. Place the dough on the hot plate and cook both sides over a medium heat. When turning the prata, add a little oil to give it a golden colour and crispy texture.

Crush the prata twice between both hands while it is still warm. Serve immediately with a curry of your choice.

Chef's Notes

- The most difficult part in making prata is flipping the dough into a paper-thin sheet, an action that takes some practice. As an alternative, use a rolling pin to flatten and stretch the dough or follow this method: place the dough on a smooth surface and flatten it into a circular shape. Using your fingers, push the dough from the centre out to the edges until you have spread it into a circle about 60-cm in diameter. Cook as described above.

- The origin of prata is traced back to India. However, the above recipe is used widely in the Malay peninsula. Roti prata is part of the common breakfast fare among locals.

MURTABAK
(ROTI PRATA WITH FILLING)

Serves 4

400 g	Mutton or chicken, minced, blanched in hot water and drained well	
¹/₂ tsp	Bryani powder	A
¹/₂ tsp	Salt	
4	Eggs	
200 g	Onions, diced	
4 tbsp	Vegetable oil	

PREPARATION AND PRESENTATION

1. Filling

   Heat the vegetable oil in a wok and fry the onions until lightly browned. Add ingredients A and fry for 8 - 10 minutes if you are using chicken and 20 - 25 minutes for mutton. Season to taste, remove from heat and set aside to cool. Mixture should be moist.

2. Dough

   Prepare the dough as in the prata recipe (see left column). Flip or roll the dough paper thin. Break an egg in the centre of the dough and spread it evenly over the central portion.

   Sprinkle a quarter of the filling onto the prata. Fold it into a rectangle. Using both hands, carefully lift the murtabak onto a well oiled hot plate. Fry until both sides are golden brown and crispy.

3. Serve immediately with a curry gravy of your choices. Other fillings such as lobster and vegetables may also be used.

Roti Prata, Traditional Indian Pancakes, and Murtabak, Indian Stuffed Pancakes served with vegetable and chicken curries.

ℋERBAL BLACK CHICKEN SOUP

A delicious and nutritious Chinese soup that is easy to prepare.

Serves 10

1 kg	Black chicken pieces
3 L	Chicken stock
To taste	Salt and pepper

Chinese Herbs

50 g	Kei chi (small red wolfer berries)
100 g	Hong zhao (red dates)
100 g	Tong sam (*Codonopsis pilosula*, dried root and a suitable ginseng substitute)
50 g	Yok chok (*Polygonatum odoraturm*, yellowish root)
50 g	Tung kwai (dried root)

PREPARATION AND PRESENTATION

Remove any excess fat and cut each chicken into 8 pieces. Blanch in boiling hot water for 1 minute to remove impurities.

Place the chicken pieces in a large porcelain container, add the herbs and chicken stock, and cover tightly. Place the container in a steamer and steam for about 1 hour. Season to taste and serve immediately while hot.

Chef's Notes

- The Chinese herbs used in this recipes are readily available in most Chinese medicine and herbal stores.
- Black chickens (Chinese black silk hens) are small birds similar to spring chickens and weigh up to 300 g when fully grown. These birds are available in most Chinese specialty stores.
- As the name suggests, black chickens are known for their black skin and dark greyish meat. They are normally only used in Chinese soup dishes. If black chicken is unavailable, spring chicken may be used. The soup will not taste the same, but the combination of double-boiling and Chinese herbs still makes it just as delicious.
- Traditionally, a nourishing soup for expectant mothers and the elderly.

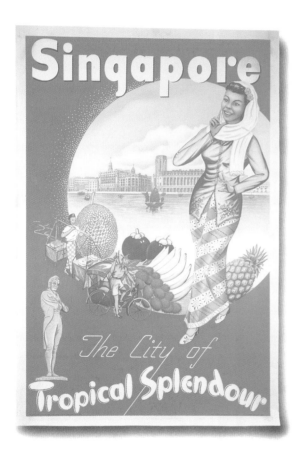

Herbal Black Chicken Soup.

SATAY WITH SPICY PEANUT SAUCE AND CONDIMENTS

A traditional Malay dish with an enduring popularity throughout Southeast Asia.

Special equipment (for ketupat): rectangular baking dish about 25-cm by 35-cm and 5-cm height.

Makes about 30 sticks

Satay

1.5 kg	Deboned chicken, beef (rump) or leg of lamb

10 g	Cumin seeds	
10 g	Coriander seeds	A
20 g	Fresh turmeric	
20 g	Lemon grass	

40 g	Sugar
10 g	Turmeric powder
30 mL	Tamarind juice
20 mL	Vegetable oil
	Salt and pepper (to taste)
100 g	Red onions, cut into squares
100 g	Cucumbers, cut into pieces with skin on
30	Bamboo skewers (about 20-cm long)

Spicy Peanut Sauce

300 g	Roasted peanuts, coarsely chopped	
20 g	Ginger	
10 g	Blue ginger	B
20 g	Lemon grass	
150 g	Shallots	
10 g	Garlic	

30 g	Sugar
150 g	Palm sugar
50 g	Dried chillies
50 g	Vegetable oil
900 mL	Tamarind juice

Ketupat/Lontong (Malay rice cakes)

500 g	Short-grain rice, unpolished
625 mL	Water
	Vegetable oil, as required
	Banana leaves

PREPARATION AND PRESENTATION

1. Satay

   Cut the meat into strips about 2-cm long and 1-cm thick. Set aside.

   Blend ingredients A in a mortar or food blender until fine.

   Place the blended mixture and the meat in a clean bowl and marinate for at least 8 hours or overnight in a refrigerator.

   Slide 5 or 6 pieces of the marinated meat onto each bamboo skewer, compacting them to about 6 - 7-cm long. Brush with oil and grill over charcoal or under a broiler until golden brown.

2. Spicy peanut sauce

   Blend ingredients B in a food processor until almost fine. Heat the oil in a saucepan and gently fry the mixture until fragrant (about 5 minutes over medium heat). Add the chilli powder, tamarind juice, sugar and palm sugar and simmer for 2 - 3 minutes. Season to taste. Remove from the heat and allow to cool. Dilute with water if required. The sauce should be fairly thick.

3. Ketupat/Lontong

   Cook the rice in a rice cooker.

   Cut two pieces of banana leaf to fit the size of the rectangular dish.

   Coat both the banana leaves and the dish with a little oil. Place one piece of banana leaf in the bottom of the dish. The banana leaves are used to give the rice a pleasant fragrance and flavour.

   Place the cooked rice on top of the banana leaf, spreading it smoothly to about 3-cm thickness.

   Place the other piece of oiled banana leaf on top of the rice and press it firmly to compress the rice. Put a heavy weight over the top of the banana leaf, ensuring that the leaf is completely covered. Leave for 2 - 3 hours, until the rice is cool and firm. Cut the rice into bite-sized squares for serving.

   Serve the satay with the spicy peanut sauce, cucumber pieces, slices of onion, and rice cakes.

Satay served the traditional way.

A "Spital Tea!"

AH TENG'S BAKERY

It isn't always easy to get a table at Ah Teng's Bakery, given that there are just six small marble-topped tables in this cosy establishment adjacent to the Empire Cafe, along busy Bras Basah Road. Here the emphasis is on robust, wholesome products and value for money.

Ah Teng's takes its name from a long-defunct Tea Room and Confectionary that once stood on nearby Victoria Street. It was as popular in the 1950s as its chief baker, Ah Teng, was famous for his adaptation of Western pastries. Here local families gathered for tea and cakes after Sunday church. English servicemen and their wives, downtown for the day from the bases in Sembawang and Changi, dropped in to buy pastries for afternoon tea. Memories of Ah Teng's delicious fare lingered long on the tastebuds of faithful patrons for many years. When plans for a bakery in the restored Raffles Hotel were first mooted, several heritage-minded Singaporeans suggested the name Ah Teng's. For old times sake. For luck.

Ah Teng's today is a thoroughly modern bakery deeply rooted in tradition. Executive Pastry Chef Roxan Villareal leads a team of 26, including six full-time bakers, who work 24 hours a day to supply over 100 items. Throughout the day trays of freshly baked classics made exclusively with fresh, natural ingredients are carried in. Fruit Cake, Banana Bread, Almond and Walnut Butter Cake, Brownies and Cheesecake, as well as Singaporean delights such as Pandan Chiffon Cake and Kueh Ubi Kaya, are brought forth to be quickly snapped up by hungry customers. The bakery does a roaring takeaway business. Displayed to tempt are traditional savouries such as chicken pies and curry puffs, and an array of freshly baked breads. Enormous cookie jars are filled each morning and emptied by the evening. The oversize Chocolate Chip Cookie is much appreciated as are the Asian Cashew Nut Cookies, Peanut Sesame Cookies and Sugee Biscuits. One can also find an excellent selection of traditional French pastries.

A more modern touch comes in the addition of items for the health conscious. The healthy Bran Muffins, for example, are one of Ah Teng's four all-time bestsellers. The others: Ham and Cheese Bun, Cheesecake and Imperial Chocolate Cake. Recipes for all these delights can be found on the pages that follow.

A sampling of the breads, cookies and pastries displayed to tempt in Ah Teng's Bakery.

KUEH LAPIS BATAVIA
(INDONESIAN LAYER CAKE)

Special equipment: 28-cm cake mould

Makes one 28-cm cake

650 g	Unsalted butter
350 g	Castor sugar
240 g	Soft flour
1/4 tsp	Salt
2 tsp	Mixed spices
4 tbsp	Brandy
10	Egg whites
36	Egg yolks

Mixed Spices

28 g	Cinnamon powder	
15 g	Clove powder	Mix together
7 g	Star anise powder	and set aside
15 g	Cardamom powder	

PREPARATION AND PRESENTATION

1. Basic cake mixture

   Sieve the soft flour and mixed spices together. In a mixer, cream the soft butter, salt and 200 g of castor sugar until light and fluffy, then slowly beat in 1 egg yolk at a time. Gradually add the brandy, flour and spice mixture.

   In another bowl, whisk the egg whites and the remaining sugar until a soft peak forms. Fold the beaten egg whites into the mixture; the egg whites should not be too stiff. Mix well with a wooden spatula.

2. Baking the cake

   Pre-heat a top-heat grill or salamander (moderate heat). Butter a piece of greaseproof paper and place it at the bottom of the cake mould. Evenly spread 1 scoop of the cake mixture on the greaseproof paper to about 1/2-cm thickness. Bake until golden brown (5 – 6 minutes). Rotate the pan while baking and use a skewer to prick any air bubbles that form.

   Repeat the process until all the cake mixture has been used. Make sure the cake surface is even before adding additional layers. When the last layer is complete, bake the cake in a pre-heated oven at 150°C for 15 minutes. Remove the cake from the pan and allow to cool for 2 – 3 hours before serving.

Chef's Notes
- Watch each layer of the cake as it bakes. The mixture will burn easily.
- Use equal amounts of mixture to produce even layers.
- Use a heavy cloth to handle the hot cake pan.

PANDAN CHIFFON CAKE

Special equipment: Baking tin 24-cm of diameter and 10-cm depth

Serves 8 - 10

150 g	Cake flour
1/2 tsp	Baking powder
1/4 tsp	Salt

Batter

8	Egg yolks
300 mL	Coconut milk, preferably fresh
2 tbsp	Fresh pandan juice
160 g	Castor sugar
1/2 tsp	Pandan essence
9	Egg whites
1 tbsp	Castor sugar
1/2 tsp	Cream of tartar

PREPARATION AND PRESENTATION

1. Batter

   Pre-heat the oven to 160°C.

   Pour the coconut milk into a saucepan and add the castor sugar. Bring to a boil, stirring slowly to dissolve the sugar. Set aside to cool.

   When the coconut mixture has cooled, sieve the cake flour, baking powder and salt. In a bowl, combine the egg yolks, coconut mixture, pandan juice and pandan essence. Whisk lightly, then add the flour to the egg yolk mixture. Mix until the batter is smooth. Set aside. Whisk the egg whites lightly and sieve in the cream of tartar and castor sugar. Continue to whisk until the mixture is stiff. Do not overbeat or allow the mixtue to become dry. Set aside.

2. Baking the cake

   Gently fold half the beaten egg whites into the egg yolk mixture and blend well. Fold in the remaining egg whites and work very lightly with a spatula. Make sure the mixture is well mixed.

   Place the finished mixture in an ungreased chiffon cake mould. Level and bake in the oven until golden brown (about 45 minutes).

   Remove the cake from the oven and invert the mould. Allow it to cool for 1 hour. Do not remove the mould while the cake is still hot.

   When it has cooled, use a long, fine palette knife to loosen the sides of the cake to remove it from the tin.

- When folding the egg whites into the batter, work lightly and do not overmix or the batter will collapse and become soggy.
- Use only clean, dry utensils when whipping the egg whites.
- The cake should be cooled for several hours before serving.
- The cake should be light green in colour.

$\mathcal{K}$UEH LAPIS
(RAINBOW LAYER CAKE)

Special equipment: Baking tin 25-cm square and 5-cm depth

Makes 1 pan

900 mL	Coconut milk, preferably fresh
270 g	Rice flour
180 g	Sago flour
¹/₄ tsp	Salt

Syrup

450 g	Sugar
150 mL	Water
6	Pandan leaves

Food Colouring

1 pinch	Yellow, red, green, brown or other natural food colourings/flavourings of your choice

Cake Tin Lining

1 piece	Banana leaf or greaseproof paper.

PREPARATION AND PRESENTATION

1. Syrup
   Add the sugar, water and pandan leaves to a clean saucepan. Bring to a boil. Simmer for 5 minutes, then remove from the heat. Discard the pandan leaves, and strain the liquid if necessary. Set aside.
2. Kueh Lapis
   Cut the banana leaf to fit the base of the cake tin, then grease it lightly with cooking oil.
   Pre-heat a steamer.
   Mix the rice, sago flour and salt in a large mixing bowl. Add the coconut milk. Use a heavy whisk to mix well.
   Stir the hot syrup into the mixture.

Divide the mixture equally into 5 bowls. Add 1 tsp of colouring to each bowl, leaving one bowl without any colouring.
Place 1 scoop of the coloured mixture in the cake tin. Steam it in a fast-boiling steamer for 6 – 7 minutes. Alternate the coloured mixture and repeat until all the batter has been used.
Remove the cake from the steamer and allow it to cool for 6 – 8 hours before serving.

- Do not refrigerate the cake as it will become hard and dry on the outside.
- This cake should never be baked in the oven.

$\mathcal{K}$UEH UBI KAYA
(TAPIOCA PANCAKES)

Makes 14 – 16

750 g	Fresh tapioca, grated
120 mL	Coconut milk, preferably fresh
120 g	Castor sugar
8	Pandan leaves
Pinch	Salt
	Vegetable oil

PREPARATION AND PRESENTATION

Pound the pandan leaves and extract the juice using a muslin or cheese-cloth.
Combine all the ingredients in a mixing bowl.
Heat a small, lightly greased non-stick pan. Spoon in the mixture until it covers the pan surface and cook over slow heat until golden brown.
Turn the pancake over and cook the other side.
Serve warm. Pancakes are enjoyed either on their own or with kaya jam, whipped sweet butter or fresh cream.

KUEH DADAH
(COCONUT PANCAKES)

Makes about 25

Pancake batter

500 mL	Coconut milk, preferably fresh
1/2 tsp	Salt
2 tbsp	Vegetable oil
4	Whole eggs
220 g	Soft flour
1 tbsp	Sago flour

Filling

600 g	Grated coconut
3 tbsp	Castor sugar
280 g	Palm sugar, chopped
4 tbsp	Water
8	Pandan leaves, knotted
1 tbsp	Sago flour

PREPARATION AND PRESENTATION

1. Filling
   Add all the ingredients except the grated coconut to a saucepan and bring to a boil. Continue to boil until the sugar dissolves.
   When the sugar has dissolved, add the grated coconut and continue to cook until the mixture becomes moist. Do not allow it to become too dry. Remove and allow to cool.
2. Pancake
   Mix all the ingredients together in a bowl, then allow to rest for 1/2 hour.
   Heat a 20-cm non-stick frying pan. Grease it lightly with cooking oil.
   Add 1 tbsp of the batter to the pan and cook over low heat. When the mixture starts to bubble, flip the pancake over to cook the other side. The pancake skin must be soft and moist. Transfer the pancake from the frying pan to a cooling rack.
   Fill each pancake with 2 tbsp of coconut filling and fold it into the shape of a pouch.
   Allow to cool and serve.

APRICOT COOKIES

Special equipment: 8-cm cake ring

Makes about 25

145 g	Butter
135 g	Brown sugar
1/2 tsp	Vanilla essence
1	Whole egg
75 g	All-purpose flour, sifted
1/4 tsp	Salt
115 g	Wheat germ
30 g	Desiccated coconut
50 g	Oats
125 g	Dried apricots, chopped coarsely
230 g	Cornflakes

PREPARATION AND PRESENTATION

Preheat the oven to 160°C.
In a large bowl, use a wooden spatula to whip the butter and sugar until soft and creamy.
Add the vanilla essence and eggs. Mix well.
Next, add the flour, salt, wheat germ, coconut, oats, chopped apricots and cornflakes. Mix well.
Take 2 tbsp of the dough and shape it into a flat, circular shape using the cake ring.
Arrange the dough on a sheet pan lightly greased with butter. Bake in the oven for 10 to 15 minutes until golden brown.
Remove from the oven and cool on a wire rack.

Chef's Note
- The cookies will remain fresh for about 1 week if kept in an air-tight container.

From left: Apple Manjari Mousse Cake, Marble Cheese Cake, Mango Cream Cake, Chocolate Truffle Cake and Imperial Chocolate Cake.

CASHEW NUT COOKIES

Makes about 70

225 g	Icing sugar
260 g	Butter
1/2	Whole egg, beaten
1	Egg yolk (for glazing)
250 g	All-purpose flour
75 g	Corn flour
450 g	Roasted cashew nuts, finely chopped
1/4 tsp	Baking soda

PREPARATION AND PRESENTATION

Preheat the oven to 160°C.

In a cake mixer bowl, combine the butter and icing sugar until soft and creamy.

Add the egg and baking soda and stir until creamy and fluffy. Add 400 g of the finely chopped cashew nuts, the all-purpose flour and the corn flour. Mix thoroughly but do not overwork or the mixture will become dry.

Take a teaspoon of the mixture and roll it into a small ball about 3-cm in diameter. Place the balls on a lightly greased sheet or nonstick pan. Leave about 2-cm between each biscuit. Place a cashew nut on each ball. With a brush, glaze each cookie with egg yolk.

Bake in the oven for 10 - 12 minutes or until light golden brown.

Remove from the oven and cool on a wire rack. Store in an airtight container. Tastes best after 2 - 3 days if you can resist the temptation.

PEANUT SESAME COOKIES

Makes about 36

125 g	Butter	
1/2 tsp	Vanilla essence	
1/2 tsp	Grated lemon	A
85 g	Sugar	
80 g	Brown sugar	
200 g	All-purpose flour	
1 tsp	Bicarbonate of soda	B
Pinch	Salt	
50 g	Sesame seeds	
125 g	Peanut butter	

PREPARATION AND PRESENTATION

Preheat the oven to 160°C.

Cream ingredients A in a large cake mixing bowl until soft and fluffy. Add the peanut butter and mix thoroughly.

Sift the flour together and add to the mixture. Mix well but do not overwork or it will become too dry.

Place the dough on a smooth work surface, lightly floured. Line a sheet pan with greaseproof paper or brush it with butter.

Roll a teaspoonful of the mixture into a ball, roll it in sesame seeds and place it on the sheet pan. Leave 5-cm between each cookie. Flatten the top slightly with your fingers.

Bake in the oven for 10 minutes until light golden brown.

Remove from the oven and cool on a wire rack. Store in an airtight container.

Clockwise from top right: Almond and Walnut Butter Cake, Fruit Cake, Kueh Lapis, Butter Cake, Sugee Biscuits, Apricot Cookies, Cashew Nut Cookies and Peanut Sesame Cookies.

SUGEE BISCUITS

Makes about 35

125 g	Ghee
95 g	Icing sugar, sifted
220 g	All-purpose flour, sifted

PREPARATION AND PRESENTATION

Preheat the oven to 160°C.

Mix the butter and icing sugar in a cake mixer bowl until soft and creamy.

Remove the bowl from the mixer and add the sifted flour. Work it with your fingertips until smooth.

Line a sheet pan with greaseproof paper or grease it lightly with butter. Take a tablespoon of the mixture at a time, shape into a ball and place on the pan.

Bake for 10 minutes until light golden brown.

Remove from the oven and cool on a wire rack. Store in an airtight container.

CREAM PUFFS WITH FRUITS

Makes about 35

Special equipment: Piping bag with a plain or star nozzle.

Choux Puffs

125 mL	Water
125 mL	Milk
100 g	Butter, cut into small pieces
3 g	Salt
5 g	Sugar
150 g	Flour, sifted
3	Eggs

Crème Patissière (Custard Pastry Cream)

6	Egg yolks
125 g	Sugar
40 g	Flour, sifted
500 mL	Milk
1	Split vanilla pod

Fruit Filling

2	Fresh kiwi	
2	Fresh mangoes	} sliced
10	Fresh strawberries	
200 g	Whipping cream	
50 g	Icing sugar	

PREPARATION AND PRESENTATION

1. Choux puffs

   Preheat the oven to 200°C.

   Put all the ingredients, except the flour and eggs, in a saucepan and boil for 1 minute over high heat, stirring with a wooden spatula. When the mixture boils, remove the pan from the heat and quickly add the sifted flour, stirring continuously to make a smooth paste. When the mixture is very smooth, return the pan to the heat and stir with a spatula for 1 minute. The paste will begin to poach and some of the water will evaporate. Be careful not to let the paste dry out too much or it will crack during cooking. Transfer the mixture to a clean bowl and allow to cool for 10 minutes.

   Add the eggs 1 at a time using a spatula. Stir well until the paste is very smooth. It is now ready to use.

   Grease a baking tray. Transfer the paste to the piping bag. Pipe the paste onto the baking tray in 5-cm circles. Continue until all the paste has been used. Place the tray in the oven. After 4 - 5 minutes, open the oven door slightly (1 - 2-cm) and leave it ajar. The cooking time will vary from 15 to 20 minutes, depending on the size of the puffs. Choux puffs are ready when they have risen and their insides have large cavities. Slight cracking may occur but this is quite normal. Remove them from the oven and allow to cool.

2. Crème patissière

   Place the egg yolks and about ⅓ of the sugar in a saucepan and whisk well. Add the flour and mix well. Set aside. Combine the milk, remaining sugar and the split vanilla pod in another saucepan and bring to a boil. As soon as the milk mixture boils, pour about ⅓ onto the egg-yolk mixture, stirring briskly all the time. Pour this back into the pan with the milk mixture and cook over low heat, stirring continuously to prevent it from burning. Allow the mixture to boil for 2 minutes, then pour the custard into a bowl. Brush a little butter over the surface or dust lightly with icing sugar to prevent a hard layer of crust from forming as the custard cools.

3. To finish and serve

   Take a knife and slice off the top ⅓ of each choux. Whisk the whipped cream to a soft peak, then fold it into the custard. Beat lightly until the cream and custard are well mixed.

   Fill a piping bag with the cream mixture and pipe it onto the choux puff.

   Arrange the sliced fruit attractively on top of the custard. Replace the top part of the choux puff. Sprinkle with icing sugar and serve.

Chef's Note

– The choux puff paste and custard can be made 1 day ahead. Store them in an airtight container.

CHEESE CAKE

Special equipment: 7.5-cm by 22-cm cake pan or spring form pan

Makes 1 cake

1 kg	Philadelphia cream cheese
280 g	Sugar
6	Eggs
90 g	Fresh cream
2 drops	Vanilla essence
1	Lemon zest (grated skin of 1 whole lemon)
1	Orange zest (grated skin of 1 whole orange)
150 g	Sour cream

PREPARATION AND PRESENTATION

Leave the cream cheese at room temperature for several hours before starting.

Preheat the oven to 160°C.

Brush the inside of the cake pan with butter and coat lightly with flour.

Place the cream cheese into a mixer bowl. Whisk at fast speed until completely creamy. Add the sugar, mix well and reduce the speed to low.

Add the whole eggs 1 at a time, followed by the vanilla essence and orange and lemon zest, stirring well to mix thoroughly.

Next, add the fresh cream followed by the sour cream. Set the speed to high to mix the ingredients completely but be careful not to overwork.

Fill the cake pan with the cheese mixture. Place the pan on a shallow tray filled with water and bake in the oven at 160°C for 1 hour.

After removing the cheese cake from the oven, leave it in the pan for 1 hour. Place the cake in a refrigerator for a further 2 – 3 hours before serving.

To serve, unmould and place on a underliner.

EXOTIC FRUIT CRUMBLE

Special equipment: 21-cm ramequin or pie dish

Makes 1 fruit crumble

Custard Cream

3	Egg yolks
60 g	Sugar
20 g	All-purpose flour
250 mL	Milk
1/2	Split vanilla pod

Crumble

220 g	All-purpose flour, sifted
110 g	Icing sugar, sifted
110 g	Butter, cut to small pieces

If using fresh fruit, select either plums, bananas, star fruit, blueberries or rhubarb.

PREPARATION AND PRESENTATION

1. Custard cream (see recipe, page 110)
2. Crumble

   Preheat the oven to 200°C.

   Pour the flour and icing sugar into a bowl and make a well in the centre.

   Add the butter pieces and work them in with your finger tips until the butter is completely mixed with the flour and icing sugar. Set aside.
3. Finishing

   Fill about 1/3 of the ramequin with custard cream.

   Arrange the sliced fruit generously on top.

   Sprinkle the crumble on top of the fruit.

   Bake in the oven at 200°C for no longer than 15 – 20 minutes. Serve warm if possible, with ice cream, whipped cream, or any other suitable fruit/berry coulis.

Truffle Cake.

MANGO CREAM CAKE

Special equipment: 22-cm diameter cake ring, piping bag with 1-cm plain nozzle, and a 25-cm cake board.

Serves 8 - 10

2	Fresh mangoes, seeded and cut into elongated slices
250 g	Mango purée (flesh of 2 ripe mangoes puréed in a blender)
75 g	Egg white
125 g	Sugar
25 mL	Cointreau liqueur
30 mL	Lemon juice
300 g	Whipped cream
5	Gelatine leaves (soaked in cold water)

Genoese Sponge

4	Whole eggs
100 g	Castor sugar
100 g	All-purpose flour, sifted
50 g	Butter, melted

Ladies' Fingers Sponge

4	Whole eggs, separated
100 g	Flour
100 g	Castor sugar

Italian Meringue

125 g	Sugar
75 g	Egg white
1/2 cup	Water

PREPARATION AND PRESENTATION

1. Genoese sponge

   Preheat the oven to 210°C.

   In a bowl, whisk the eggs and sugar with a balloon whisk. Continue until the mixture is light and creamy, and has doubled in volume.

   Gently fold in the flour and the melted butter. Ensure that the flour and butter are thoroughly mixed. Place the mixture in a greased and floured cake ring. Bake in the oven for approximately 30 minutes.

   To check whether the sponge is ready, insert a skewer or the point of a very fine knife into the centre; it should come out clean.

   Take the sponge from the oven, remove the cake ring and allow to cool on a wire rack.

2. Ladies' fingers sponge

   Pre-heat the oven to 210°C.

   Before starting this step, line a large baking tray with greaseproof paper and place cake ring in the centre. Cream the egg yolks and 50 g of the sugar in a bowl. Whip the egg whites until stiff, then add a little of the white and mix thoroughly.

   Gradually add the sieved flour and the remainder of the egg whites alternately folding as lightly as possible. Place the mixture in a piping bag with a 1-cm plain tube and pipe small (about 2-cm) balls next to each other until the greaseproof paper is covered completely. Using a sieve, sprinkle the balls liberally with icing sugar.

   Bake in the oven for approximately 10 minutes. Remove from the oven and allow to cool. Set aside.

3. Italian meringue

   Place the sugar in a saucepan. Add sufficient water to melt the sugar. Allow to simmer steadily on low heat without stirring. Continue heating until the water reduces, leaving a sticky, pliable residue. Remove from the heat.

   Whip the egg whites until stiff and pour in the sugar syrup. Continue to whip until the mixture rises and doubles in volume. Leave in the bowl.

4. Mango Cream Cake

   Drain the gelatine leaves and place them in a saucepan. Add the Cointreau and lemon juice, and heat very gently to dissolve the gelatine. Do not allow to boil! Fold the mango purée into the gelatine mixture and stir. Next, add the Italian meringue, fold in the whipped cream and mix very gently.

5. Cut the sponge in half horizontally. Put one piece on a cake board and place the cake ring over it. (Use the other half of the sponge for a second cake.) Arrange fresh mango slices on top of the sponge, then fill the cake ring to the top with mango mousse. Carefully smooth the surface with a palette knife.

   Put the Ladies' Fingers Sponge on top of the mango mousse and leave in the refrigerator for a minimum of 5 hours or until set.

6. When ready to serve, remove the cake ring and sprinkle the surface with icing sugar.

CHOCOLATE AND RASPBERRY ROLL

Special equipment: 20-cm by 30-cm tray
Serves 8 - 10

Chocolate Sponge

100 g	Butter
100 g	Castor sugar
135 g	Egg yolk
20 g	Corn starch
80 g	Flour, sifted
35 g	Cocoa powder
35 g	Roasted hazelnuts, finely chopped
200 g	Egg white
35 g	Icing sugar

Raspberry Jelly

500 g	Raspberry purée
375 g	Castor sugar
25 g	Glucose
7 g	Pectin powder

White Chocolate Mousse

125 g	White chocolate, melted	} mixed
250 g	Whipped cream	together

Dark Chocolate Glaze

100 mL	Milk
25 g	Sugar
35 g	Glucose
160 g	Dark chocolate, cut into small pieces

PREPARATION AND PRESENTATION

1. Sponge
   In a cake mixer, cream the butter and sugar until smooth then add the egg yolks, one at a time, until the mixture is fluffy. Transfer the mixture to a large bowl and set aside. Beat the egg whites well until they rise, then add the sugar and beat faster for 1 minute.
   Sieve the corn starch, cocoa powder, hazelnuts and flour together and set aside.
   Add ⅓ of the egg whites to the butter mixture and mix thoroughly using a flat spatula. Then add the sifted ingredients, mix thoroughly and add the remaining egg whites.
   Use a palette knife to spread this mixture to a thickness of 3 - 5 mm over a sheet pan that has been lightly buttered and floured, or lined with greaseproof paper. Bake immediately in the oven for 8 minutes at 230°C. To test whether the sponge is ready for use, touch it with your fingertips. It should be firm and moist but not stick to your fingers.
   Slide the sponge onto a wire rack. Remove the greaseproof paper just before using.

2. Raspberry jelly
   Place the raspberry purée in a saucepan and bring it to a boil. When the raspberry purée boils, add the glucose, sugar and pectin, stirring constantly to ensure that the ingredients are completely dissolved.
   Stop stirring and allow to boil for 1 minute. Remove from the heat and allow to cool and set.
   When the mixture has cooled and thickened, remove the greaseproof paper from the sponge. Flip the sponge over onto another piece of greaseproof paper. Smoothen the raspberry jelly evenly over the entire sponge surface with a palette knife.
   Chill for 10 minutes.

3. White chocolate mousse
   Melt the chopped white chocolate. When cooled slightly, fold in the cream.

4. Dark chocolate glaze
   Bring the milk, sugar and glucose to a boil. Place the chocolate pieces in a bowl and slowly pour in the milk mixture. Stir well and ensure that the chocolate pieces are completely dissolved and the mixture is of a smooth consistency. This glaze can be prepared 1 day in advance.

5. Finishing
   Remove the chilled sponge and carefully smoothen the white chocolate mousse over it. Slowly roll up the sponge, taking care not to tear it.
   Pour the dark chocolate glaze over the entire roll.
   Chill for 1 hour to set. Remove after the chocolate sets and slice before serving.

Clockwise from top right: Ivory Flower, Cheops Pyramid and Cream Puffs with Fruits.

IMPERIAL CHOCOLATE CAKE

Special equipment: 22-cm diameter cake ring, 25-cm square cake board.

Makes one 22-cm cake

40 g	Sugar	⎫
30 g	Water	⎬ Sugar Syrup
3	Egg yolks	⎭

Italian Meringue (see recipe, page 112)

3	Egg whites
80 g	Sugar
3	Gelatine leaves, soaked in cold water
170 g	Bitter chocolate, cut into small pieces
330 g	Whipped cream
1	Kueh Lapis Batavia cake cut into ½-cm by 3-cm by 5-cm slices (see recipe, page 104)
2 slices	Chocolate sponge (see recipe, page 113, remove 20 g of the flour and add 20 g of cocoa powder)

Rum Syrup

25 g	Sugar
50 mL	Water
25 mL	Rum

Glaze

100 g	Chocolate, cut into small pieces and softened
200 g	Fresh cream (unwhipped)

PREPARATION AND PRESENTATION

1. Chocolate cake

   Place the cake ring on the cake board. Very lightly grease the sides of the ring with butter. Line the inner part of the cake ring with the kueh lapis slices (about 2.5-cm high), then place one slice of the chocolate sponge inside the circular ring of kueh lapis.

   Boil the sugar and water in a saucepan until a very thick syrup forms.

   Place the egg yolks in a bowl and whisk. When the sugar syrup is ready, pour it onto the yolks and whisk well until the mixture is thick and creamy. Set aside in a warm place.

2. Prepare the Italian meringue as described on page 112.

3. Gelatine mixture

   Strain the gelatine leaves and pour them into the hot meringue. Stir until the gelatine has completely dissolved.

   Melt the bitter chocolate in a double boiler or microwave at medium heat for 2 minutes.

   Using a large bowl, combine the melted chocolate and the mixture of yolks and sugar syrup. Stir well and incorporate the Italian meringue and gelatine mixture. Stir well to mix, then fold in the whipped cream.

   Pour half the mixture into the cake ring, insert the second layer of chocolate sponge and soak it with the rum syrup.

   If you do not wish to use rum, you may substitute with Grand Marnier or Cointreau.

   Completely fill the ring with the chocolate mixture. Use a palette knife to smoothen the surface. Leave the ring in the refrigerator overnight.

4. Finishing

   In a saucepan, incorporate the chocolate and the cream over low heat. Remove the saucepan from the heat and stir the mixture until it is completely smooth.

   Pour the ganache over the top of the cake and use a palette knife to smoothen the surface, working fast before the glaze has time to set. A quick hand is essential.

   When the entire surface is covered, leave the glaze to set, then remove the cake ring. Ready to serve.

High tea in the Sarkies Suite. From left: Pandan Chiffon Cake, Chicken Pie, Durian Mousse Cake, Croissant and Bread Pudding, and Tapioca Pancakes. On the carrier, Fruit Tartlettes, Scones and French Pastries..

CHOCOLATE WITH HAZELNUTS IN CHINESE TEACUPS

Makes 10 Chinese miniature teacups

125 g	Praline paste
15 g	Hazelnut gianduja, chopped into small pieces
160 g	Milk chocolate, chopped into small pieces
30 g	Roasted hazelnuts, skinless

PREPARATION AND PRESENTATION

Place the milk chocolate and hazelnut gianduja pieces in a bowl and melt in a double boiler or microwave for 2 minutes at medium heat. Add the praline paste and stir until smooth and completely mixed. Fill 1/3 of each Chinese teacup with the chocolate ganache. Add a few pieces of roasted hazelnut. Pour more of the ganache to within about 1-cm of the rim. Decorate each teacup with one hazelnut. Allow the chocolate to set for about 1 hour before serving.

CHOCOLATE WITH RAISINS IN CHINESE TEACUPS

Makes 10 Chinese miniature teacups

100 g	Milk chocolate, chopped into small pieces
100 g	Dark chocolate, chopped into small pieces
40 mL	Evaporated milk
40 mL	Water
6 g	Tea leaves, Earl Grey
20 g	Raisins
2 tbsp	Dark rum

PREPARATION AND PRESENTATION

Soak the raisins in rum overnight.
Add the tea leaves and water to a saucepan, and bring to a boil. Remove from the heat and cover for 1/2 hour. Strain the tea into another saucepan.
Pour the evaporated milk into the tea and bring to a boil. Remove the saucepan from the heat and set aside. Melt the milk and dark chocolates in a double boiler or microwave for 2 minutes at medium setting. Add the melted chocolate to the tea and milk mixture. Stir well with a wooden spatula until smooth. Fill 1/3 of a Chinese teacup with the ganache, then add some soaked raisins and cover with more ganache. Allow the chocolate to set for about 1 hour before serving.

TRUFFLE CAKE

Special equipment: Cake ring of 20-cm diameter, 11-cm height

Makes 1 cake

500 g	Whipped cream
2	Egg yolks
200 g	Dark chocolate, cut into pieces
100 g	Sugar
50 mL	Water
100 g	Raisins
40 mL	Dark rum
30 g	Fine icing sugar
50 g	Cocoa powder
1	Chocolate sponge (see recipe, page 113)

PREPARATION AND SERVING

1. Raisins and sugar syrup
   Soak the raisins in hot water for 30 minutes, then strain. Pour into a bowl, add the rum and leave overnight. To make the sugar syrup, dissolve the sugar in boiling water and set aside to cool.
2. Truffle cake
   Place the cake ring on a cake board. Cut a slice of chocolate sponge 1-cm thick and 1-cm less in diameter than the ring. Strain the raisins, pouring the rum into the sugar syrup. Use a brush to baste the sponge with this mixture. Scatter the raisins on top of the sponge. Melt the chocolate pieces in a double boiler or microwave at medium heat for 2 minutes. Carefully fold half of the whipped cream into the melted chocolate and whisk until smooth. Add the remaining whipped cream and whisk well. Fill the cake ring with the mixture, levelling the surface with a flat spatula. Place in the refrigerator for two hours. When cake has set, carefully remove the ring. Before serving, cover the surface completely with a thin coating of icing sugar, followed by another layer of cocoa powder.

Chinese teacups filled with chocolate, hazelnuts and chocolate raisins.

GATEAU BERNARD

Serves 8 to 12

500 g	Flour
10 g	Salt
10 g	Sugar
3	Whole eggs
200 mL	Water
15 g	Fresh yeast
175 g	Butter
600 g	Custard cream (see recipe, page 110)

Almond Topping

200 g	Butter
150 g	Honey
100 g	Sugar
50 g	Glucose
1	Lemon zest (grated skin of 1 whole lemon)
1	Orange zest (grated skin of 1 whole orange)
300 g	White almonds, sliced

PREPARATION AND PRESENTATION

1. Dough

   In a cake mixer fitted with a dough hook or K blade, mix all the ingredients except the butter and shortening at slow speed for 2 minutes and at high speed for 6 minutes.

   When the dough is ready, place it on a lightly floured surface and allow it to rest for 30 minutes.

2. Almond topping

   Preheat the oven to 210°C.

   In a saucepan, bring the butter, honey, sugar, glucose and zests to a boil. Then add the white almonds and use a wooden spatula to mix thoroughly. Allow to cool.

   In the meantime, evenly spread the dough into a 40-cm diameter circle, 2-cm thick, on large, flat baking pan. When the almond topping mixture cools, spread it as evenly as possible over the top of the dough.

   Bake the cake in the oven for 25 to 30 minutes.

   To check if the gateau is ready, insert the point of a very fine knife into the centre. It should come out clean. Remove from the oven and allow to cool.

   When cool, slice in half horizontally using a long cake knife. Evenly spread the custard cream to about 1-cm thickness over the bottom half. Replace the top half and slice the cake into the desired portions.

Chef's Note

– You can add raisins or mixed dried fruits to the custard cream for variety.

FRUIT CAKE

Special equipment: Two loaf pans, 25-cm long, 10-cm wide and 7-cm deep

Makes 2 loaves

300 g	Butter
100 g	Castor sugar
100 g	Brown sugar
6	Whole eggs
400 g	Black raisins

400 g	Golden raisins	
100 g	Orange peel	
100 g	Lemon peel	
100 g	Red cherries	A
100 g	Green cherries	
1/2 cup	Orange juice	
1/2 cup	Lemon juice	

300 g	All-purpose flour, sifted
30 g	Glucose
150 g	Apricot glaze
2 tbsp	Dark rum, optional

PREPARATION AND PRESENTATION

Combine ingredients A and leave to marinate overnight. Preheat the oven to 200°C.

In a cake mixer, cream the butter, castor and brown sugar until light and fluffy.

Add the whole eggs one at a time.

Continue beating until well mixed. Add marinated ingredients A. Mix well.

Next add the flour and glucose, stir well and remove from the mixer.

Pour the mixture into a loaf pan lined with aluminum foil or baking paper. Place in the oven for 10 minutes. Reduce the heat to about 150°C and continue baking for about 1 hour. To check if the cake is ready, insert the point of a very fine knife into the centre. It should come out clean.

ℬANANA BREAD

Special equipment: Two loaf pans, 25-cm long, 10-cm wide and 7-cm deep

Makes 2 loaves

450 g	Ripe banana, peeled
450 g	Sugar
4	Eggs
15 g	Baking soda, sifted
190 mL	Milk
125 g	Corn oil
450 g	All-purpose flour, sifted
3 drops	Vanilla essence

PREPARATION AND PRESENTATION

Blend the banana and sugar at low speed in a mixer until completely smooth. Add the eggs 1 at a time, followed by the baking soda, milk, corn oil and vanilla essence. Continue to mix at medium speed for 5 minutes or until all the ingredients are very smooth, occasionally scraping the sides of the bowl.

Reduce the mixer speed to low and add the all-purpose flour. Mix well.

Brush the pans with butter and fill to ³/₄ full with the banana mixture.

Bake the banana bread at 160°C for 1 hour and 10 minutes.

To check if the bread is ready, insert a skewer or the point of a very fine knife into the centre. It should come out clean.

Remove the bread from the oven and unmold immediately. Place on a wire rack and allow to cool thoroughly before serving.

𝒜LMOND AND WALNUT BUTTER CAKE

Special equipment: Two loaf pans, 25-cm long, 10-cm wide and 7-cm deep

Makes 2 loaves

330 g	Butter	
300 g	Sugar	} A
3 drops	Vanilla essence	
6	Whole eggs	
290 g	All-purpose flour, sifted	} B
10 g	Baking powder, sifted	
75 g	Almonds, cut into strips	
75 g	Walnuts, chopped coarsely	

PREPARATION AND PRESENTATION

Preheat the oven to 200°C.

Combine ingredients A in a cake mixer bowl and mix until creamy. Do not overwork!

Add the eggs one at a time and continue stirring until well mixed.

Sift the flour and baking powder together, then fold into mixture A.

Remove the bowl from the cake mixer, add the almond slices and walnuts, and stir with a wooden spatula. (Save a few almonds and walnuts for decoration.) Brush the inside of the loaf pan with butter. Pour in mixture A (sprinkle the remaining almonds and walnuts on top) and bake in the oven for about 10 minutes, then reduce the temperature to 160°C and continue baking for another hour.

To check whether the cake is ready, insert a skewer or the point of a very fine knife into the centre. It should come out clean.

Remove the cake from the oven and leave in the loaf pan for 5 to 10 minutes, unmould on a wire rack.

Allow to cool for several hours before serving. Serve thinly sliced, on its own.

BLUEBERRY MUFFINS

Special equipment: Standard muffin tray and paper muffin cups

Makes about 8 to 10

90 g	Butter
100 g	Sugar
2	Whole eggs
120 mL	Milk
215 g	Cake flour, sifted
63 g	Egg white
10 g	Baking powder, sifted
100 g	Blueberry, preferably fresh

PREPARATION AND PRESENTATION

Preheat the oven to 180°C.

Use a cake mixer to whisk the butter and sugar until smooth and creamy. Add the whole eggs one at a time, followed by the milk. Scrape the sides of the bowl occasionally.

Sift the flour and baking powder together and add them to the mixture, followed by the egg whites. Be careful not to overwork this dough. Remove the bowl from the mixer and incorporate the blueberries using a wooden spatula.

Line the muffin trays with the paper cups. Use a spoon to fill each cup with the mixture.

Bake in the oven for 20 minutes at 180°C.

To check whether the muffins are ready, insert a skewer or the point of a fine knife into the centre. It should come out clean.

Leave the muffins on the trays for 5 minutes, then unmould them onto a wire rack and serve warm.

Chef's Note

– To make walnut and coffee muffins, add 2 drops of coffee essence and 80 g of chopped walnuts instead of the blueberries.

BRAN MUFFINS

Special equipment: Standard muffin tray and paper muffin cups

Makes about 8 to 10

90 g	Brown sugar	⎫
95 mL	Vegetable oil	⎬ A
50 mL	Honey	
10 mL	Molasses	
8 g	Baking soda	⎭
Pinch	Salt	
90 g	Wholemeal flour	
70 g	Cake flour	
70 g	Bran flakes	
25 g	High-protein flour or bread flour	
95 g	Eggs	
140 mL	Milk	
70 g	Raisins	
30 g	Pineapple, preferably fresh, chopped into small pieces	

PREPARATION AND PRESENTATION

Preheat the oven to 180°C.

Combine ingredients A well, then add the eggs, milk and mix thoroughly.

Add the flour (cake flour, protein flour, wholemeal flour) and mix well for 1 minute. Add the bran flakes, raisins and chopped pineapple. Mix well.

Line the muffin tray with the paper cups. Use a spoon to fill each cup to the rim.

Bake in the oven at 180°C for 20 minutes or until done. Do not under-bake.

To check whether the bran muffins are ready, insert a skewer or the point of a fine knife into the centre. It should come out clean.

Leave the muffins on the trays for 5 minutes, then unmould onto a wire rack and serve warm.

HAM AND CHEESE BUNS

Makes about 5

500 g	Bread flour
100 g	Herbed cream cheese
300 g	Ham, thinly sliced
5 g	Salt
50 g	Sugar
25 g	Fresh yeast
35 g	Butter
25 mL	Milk
200 mL	Water ⎫
1	Whole egg ⎬ Combine

PREPARATION AND PRESENTATION

In a cake mixer fitted with a dough hook or K blade, combine all the ingredients except the butter and mix at low speed for 2 minutes and at high speed for 6 minutes. Transfer the dough to a smooth working surface and cover with a damp cloth. Allow to rest for 10 minutes. On a lightly floured surface, roll out the dough to about 1-cm thick. Cut five 13-cm square pieces. Spread about 20 g of herb cream cheese evenly over each piece, then place about 60 g of ham on the cheese (use more cheese or ham if desired).
Roll up each of the dough pieces, then fold them in half and pinch the ends together. Place the dough seam-side down on the working surface and make a 7-cm incision to expose the cheese and ham.
Place on a baking tray and cover with a damp cloth. Allow to rest for 30 minutes. Preheat the oven to 180°C. Brush each piece of dough with the egg mixture and bake in the oven for 12 - 15 minutes.
When ready, remove from the oven. Best enjoyed when served warm.

BANANA COUNTRYSIDE

Special equipment: 22-cm shallow pie dish, 3-cm depth

Serves 8 to 10

Dough
Use the same dough as the recipe for the Ham and Cheese Bun (above).

Crumble
Use the same crumble as the recipe for the Exotic Fruit Crumble on page 111.

Almond Cream

Yields about 550 g

125 g	Butter
125 g	Fine sugar
125 g	Almond powder
25 g	Flour
3	Small eggs

PREPARATION AND PRESENTATION

1. Almond cream
   With a spatula, work the butter until soft, then add the sugar, almond powder and flour and mix thoroughly. Add the eggs, one at a time, beat the mixture after each addition. Continue until mixture is light and homogenous.
2. To finish and serve
   Preheat the oven to 200°C.
   On a lightly floured surface, roll the dough into a circular shape about 5 mm thick.
   Lightly grease the pie dish and place dough on the base. With your fingertips, lightly pinch up the edges of the dough around the pie dish.
   Evenly spread a thin layer of the almond cream over the base of the dough. Arrange a generous amount of bananas on top of the almond cream, covering it completely. Sprinkle a layer of the crumble over the bananas. Set aside for half an hour.
   Lower the temperature of the oven to 170°C and bake dish for half an hour.
   Remove the dish from the oven and allow to cool.
   Serve warm or cold with fruit coulis or whipped cream.

Chef's Note
- The almond cream will remain fresh for 4 - 5 days if stored in an air-tight container and chilled. Remove from the chiller half an hour before using.

Banana Countryside, Assortment of Ah Teng's Muffins and Gateau Bernard.

PLAITED BREAD
(FARMER'S PLAIT)

Makes 1 loaf

500 g	Bread flour
100 g	Yeast
100 g	Sugar
5 g	Salt
1	Egg
50 g	Butter
50 g	Vegetable shortening
100 mL	Condensed milk
100 mL	Water

PREPARATION AND PRESENTATION
1. Dough
   Make the dough as described for Gateau Bernard, page 123. Divide the dough into two equal pieces and allow to rest for 15 minutes.
2. Plaiting the dough
   Preheat the oven to 180°C.
   Roll both pieces of dough out to about 80-cm long. Ensure that the strands are of equal consistency and shape when rolled.
   Place the dough strands one over the other in the shape of an X, then plait the strands accordingly.
   When the plait is ready, brush with the egg mixture and bake for 20 minutes.
   Remove the loaf from the oven and allow to cool before serving.

TROPICAL SCONES

Special equipment: 6-cm cookie cutter

Makes about 18

65 g	Sugar
65 g	Butter
1	Egg
450 g	Flour, sifted
30 g	Baking powder, sifted
250 mL	Milk
65 g	Raisins (optional)
1	Egg, beaten (for glazing)

PREPARATION AND PRESENTATION
Preheat the oven to 200°C.
Combine the butter and sugar in a cake mixer. Mix until fluffy and creamy, then add the egg.

Add the flour and baking powder and mix until a crumble forms.
Pour in the milk and mix to a smooth texture. Do not overwork as the mixture will toughen. Add the raisins.
Lightly flour a smooth surface and roll out the dough to about 3-cm thick. Use the cookie cutter to cut out individual pieces. Glaze with the egg mixture.
Place the scones on a baking sheet and bake in the oven for 10 minutes or until golden brown.
Remove from the oven, allow to cool and serve, ideally, with kaya, jam, clotted cream, farm-fresh butter and a hot pot of tea.

Chef's Note
– The best scones are made when you mix the dough by hand. The dough must stay light and fluffy.

RAFFLES BREAD AND CROISSANT PUDDING

Fills 1 medium-sized oven-proof porcelain dish

10-12 slices	Bread and leftover croissants
250 mL	Milk
250 mL	Fresh cream
150 g	Sugar
3	Whole eggs
2 drops	Vanilla essence
50 g	Butter, cut into small pieces

PREPARATION AND PRESENTATION
Preheat the oven to 150°C.
Place all the ingredients except the bread, croissant slices and butter into a bowl and mix well with a whisk.
Grease the oven-proof dish with butter and sprinkle with a little sugar. Arrange the bread and croissant slices in the dish and fill with the milk mixture.
Place several pieces of butter flakes on top of the bread. Allow to soak for about 20 minutes.
Place the dish in a large baking tray half-filled with water and bake in the oven for 30 minutes. Do not allow the water to get into the pudding.

From left: Vegetarian Curry Puffs, Ham and Cheese Buns and Plaited Bread

Chapter Five

THE EMPRESS ROOM

The Empress Room has been a welcome addition to Raffles Hotel's restaurants, earning a following among Singaporeans and visitors alike for its fine Cantonese food. The decor is warm and calming, and has a deliberately residential air: terracotta-tiled floors, old-fashioned lace curtains, timber panels and ceiling, and simple white china and blackwood chopsticks set out on pale peach tablecloths.

Of all China's cooking styles, Cantonese cuisine is considered the most refined and, because the Cantonese were the first to emigrate in large numbers in the mid-19th century, it is the best known outside of China. The emphasis is on fresh ingredients and quick stir-frying and steaming in order to preserve nutrients and natural flavours. Cantonese chefs, traditionally a breed of highly specialized craftsmen dedicated to polishing and improving their art, are also known for the frequent use of nuts and mushrooms in their dishes, as well as seafood and roasted or grilled pork and poultry.

As with all Chinese food, a well prepared Cantonese dish is expected to appeal to more than the one sense of taste. Its colours should be pleasing to the eye, the ingredients should be of uniform size, and it should be fragrant. There should be contrasting tastes and textures within the meal: if one dish is crisp, it should be offset by another that is smooth; a spicy dish should be paired with a dish that is neutral.

One can eat simply in the Empress Room or indulge in such luxuries as braised abalone, shark's fin and bird's nest. In a formal Chinese banquet which is served in nine or ten courses, the arrival of any of these foods on the table is considered a highlight of the evening. The birds' nests used are made by swiftlets that construct them with gelatinous matter. Shark's fin is sold in its dried form and shape, and cooked in chicken stock. The intricate preparation needed for both dishes, combined with the rarity of their main ingredients, lends them enormous prestige.

The kitchen is presided over by chef Banson Yeung and his team, who are also responsible for the Chinese banquets served in the hotel's function rooms. Here the chefs share a selection of appetizers, soups, entrées, vegetables and desserts from among the Empress Room's most popular dishes.

An Empress Room
waitress oversees a display of
Chinese teas.

STIR-FRIED LOBSTER WITH GARLIC AND CHILLI

Serves 10

2	Rock lobsters (700 - 800 g each)
2 tbsp	Cornflour
1.6 L	Vegetable oil
1	Red chilli, diced with seeds removed
6	Garlic cloves, finely minced
1/2 tsp	Garlic salt
1 1/2 tsp	Chinese rice wine (hua tiao jiou)

} A

PREPARATION AND PRESENTATION

Cut antennae, feelers and legs to within 4-cm from the body, wash thoroughly under running water. Leave the shell on and cut each lobster into 10 pieces.
Rinse lobster pieces again thoroughly, drain and pat dry with absorbent paper towels. Lightly but evenly, cover lobster pieces with cornflour.
Heat wok and add oil, stir-fry lobster till completely cooked, approximately 4 - 5 minutes. Remove and place fried lobster pieces on absorbent paper towels. Drain excess oil from wok, leaving a little to stir-fry ingredients A for 1 - 2 minutes. Add fried lobster pieces and toss for about 1 - 2 minutes longer or until all the pieces are well coated with the fragrant and spicy mixture. Remove and serve immediately.

Chef's Note
– A dish that is light and easily prepared yet adds a touch of exotic glamour to any meal.

BRAISED SUPERIOR SHARK'S FIN WITH SUPREME BROTH

Serves 10

600 g	Superior shark's fin, processed
1.2 kg	Lean pork (shoulder)
1.2 kg	Chicken
3 L	Water
2 tbsp	Vegetable oil
1 tsp	Chinese rice wine (hua tiao jiou)
2 tsp	Salt
8 tbsp	Cornflour mixture (1 part flour to 4 parts water)

Garnish

100 g	Yunnan ham, shredded
300 g	Beansprouts
200 mL	Water
1 tbsp	Light soya sauce

PREPARATION AND PRESENTATION

1. Supreme broth
   Place 1 kg of lean pork, 1 kg of chicken and 3 L of water in a pot. Bring to a boil and simmer for 4 hours. Season to taste with salt.
   Strain the stock.
2. Shark's Fin
   Cook 200 g each of the lean pork and chicken in a portion of the prepared stock until tender. Remove and shred finely. Place 60 g of superior shark's fin in a stainless-steel bowl. Place the shredded pork and chicken on top of the shark's fin. Add enough stock to totally immerse the shark's fin and the meat. Wrap the bowl tightly with plastic wrap and place it in a steamer for 45 minutes. When done, remove the shredded chicken and lean pork. Place the shark's fin in a serving bowl. Set aside.
3. Sauce
   Pour 200 mL of the prepared stock into a wok and bring to high heat. Add the Chinese wine and oil, and boil. Add salt to taste.
4. To finish and serve
   Spread the sauce and shredded Yunnan ham over the shark's fin.
   Blanch the beansprouts in water, oil and soya sauce, drain. Place the cooked beansprouts in the wok and add one teaspoon of oil and 1/2 teaspoon of salt. Toss and place on a separate plate. Sprinkle a little shredded ham over the beansprouts. To serve, beansprouts are added to the shark's fin at the last moment.

Braised Superior Shark's Fin with Supreme Broth.

Chef's Notes

– Although processed shark's fin is now widely available, the chefs at Raffles prepare it in the following manner:
The shark's fin is washed under cold running water, then soaked in cold water for 24 hours. The texture becomes soft and jelly-like.
The water is drained and the shark's fin are placed, piece by piece, between two bamboo nets. The sides are tied with loosely-woven bamboo strips. This ensures that the shark's fin does not break apart during simmering.
The shark's fin is then simmered in water for 4 hours. The water is changed and the shark's fin is simmered again for another 4 hours. This is known as a cleansing process. During the last 30 minutes of the second 4 hours, ginger juice is added. The shark's fin is removed from the water and spread out evenly on a plate. When cool, the fins are ready for cooking.

$\mathcal{B}$ARBECUED PEKING DUCK

1	Duck, 2.5 kg	

Marinade for interior of duck carcass

1 tsp	Sugar	
2 tsp	Salt	A
1/2 tsp	Five-spice powder	
1/2 tsp	Ginger powder	

Seasoning

30 g	Old ginger	
3	Star anise	B
1	Bay leaf	

Basting sauce

10 g	Maltose sugar	
5 mL	Chinese red vinegar	
30 mL	Rice vinegar	C
10 mL	Chinese red rice wine (Shao hsing hue tiao jiou)	

Sauce

30 g	Sugar	
1 tsp	Oyster sauce	
2 tbsp	Fermented soya bean paste	
3 tbsp	Hoisin paste	D
2 tbsp	Sesame paste	
1 tbsp	Oil	

Garnish

22	Spring onions, stems only
2	Red chillies, sliced into 3-mm rings
22	Egg-skin pancakes

PREPARATION AND PRESENTATION

1. Peking duck sauce
   Mix all ingredients D except the oil. Heat the oil in a saucepan, pour in ingredients D and bring to a boil, stirring well. Remove from the heat and allow to cool.

2. Duck
   Remove the innards, wash thoroughly and drain.
   Marinate the inside of the duck with ingredients A. Do not use this on the skin. Allow to stand for 20 minutes.
   Place ingredients B inside the duck. Seal with a skewer. Immerse the entire duck in rapidly boiling water for 5 seconds. Remove and immediately dip into ice-cold water for about 5 seconds, remove and pat dry.
   Mix ingredients C and baste the skin. This gives Peking Duck its succulent dark-brown appearance.
   Hang the duck in a cool, well-ventilated place for about 6 hours.

3. Roasting the duck and slicing the skin
   Preheat the oven to 150°C.
   Roast the duck, breast side up for 20 minutes, then turn over and roast for further 15 minutes. Remove from the oven and allow to cool slightly. Slice the skin off the duck into 22 pieces (see *Chef's Notes*).

4. Garnish
   Wash the spring onions in water. Dry and slice the stem into 2-cm lengths.
   Place the 22 egg-skins, overlapping each other, on a round plate. Seal tightly with a piece of plastic wrap and steam for 5 minutes.
   Remove the wrap and serve the egg-skins, spring onions and sauce alongside with the Peking Duck skins.

Chef's Notes

– To slice the skin from the duck, place the carcass on a chopping board breast side up. With a sharp knife, first slit the flesh along the breast bone, then along the edge of the rib cage on both sides. Next, make a series of horizontal cuts outwards from the breast bone.

– Turn the duck over and make similar incisions on the other side.

– Only the skin of the duck is used; the remainder can be used to prepare other dishes such as fried rice.

– Egg-skin pancakes may be purchased ready-made at Chinese specialty stores.

Barbecued Peking Duck.

BRAISED ABALONE AND SEA CUCUMBER WITH BABY KAILAN

Serves 10

10	Dried abalone (approx. 30 g per piece)
400 mL	Clear chicken stock
2 tbsp	Chinese rice wine (red)
4 tbsp	Cornflour paste
400 g	Baby kailan
100 mL	Vegetable oil
500 mL	Water
1 tsp	Sugar
1 tsp	Salt
1 tbsp	Light soya sauce
400 g	Fresh sea cucumbers, pre-soaked and cut into 1-cm by 2-cm pieces
2 tbsp	Vegetable oil
1	Garlic clove, peeled
1 L	Clear chicken stock
30 g	Ginger, sliced
30 g	Spring onions, sliced
3 tbsp	Oyster sauce

PREPARATION AND PRESENTATION

1. Sea cucumbers
   Heat a wok, add the oil and stir-fry the garlic and ginger for 2 minutes. Add the stock, spring onions, oyster sauce and sea cucumbers and bring to a boil. Allow to simmer for 1/2 an hour over medium heat. When the sea cucumbers are soft, remove them from the heat and set aside.
2. Baby kailan
   Heat a wok and add the oil, water, sugar and salt and bring to a boil. Add the baby kailan and cook for about 4 - 5 minutes. Drain, add the soya sauce and toss. Arrange the baby kailan around the rim of a large serving plate.
3. Abalone
   Heat a wok and add the stock and sea cucumbers, and cook for 5 minutes. Add the abalone and Chinese wine, and thicken with the cornflour mixture if required. Season to taste.
4. Serving
   Place the sea cucumbers in the centre of the serving plate, arrange the abalone and serve immediately.

Chef's Notes

- Canned abalone may be used as a substitute. However, the chefs at Raffles Hotel prepare the dried abalone for cooking in the following manner:
  Dried abalone is soaked in cold water for 24 hours, after which the water is changed and boiled for 2 hours. Then the abalone is cleaned by hand and washed again to remove remaining impurities.
  Next, 1.2 kg each of chicken, lean pork and Yunnan ham, 600 g of oyster sauce, 300 g of white rock sugar are placed in a cooking pot. The abalone is added and the pot is filled with water to 5-cm above the ingredients. It is then stewed for 8 hours, after which the abalone is ready for cooking.
- Sea cucumber may be purchased pre-soaked at Chinese specialty foodstores.

STEAMED RED GROUPER WITH BLACK BEAN SAUCE

Serves 10

1 kg	Freshest red grouper fillet, cut into 10
1/2 tsp	Salt
40 mL	Black bean sauce
40 g	Ginger, minced
40 g	Garlic, minced
1	Dried mandarin-orange peel, minced
1 tsp	Sugar
1 tsp	Sesame oil

(A)

Garnish

100 g	Spring onions, sliced
20 g	Chinese parsley, leaves only

Sauce

100 mL	Vegetable oil
2 tbsp	Light soya sauce

PREPARATION AND PRESENTATION

Gently rub the salt on the fish fillets.
Mix ingredients A and pour the mixture over the fish. Steam over high heat for 12 - 15 minutes. Place on a serving dish.
Heat a wok, add the oil and soya sauce, and stir. Pour this mixture over the steamed fish.
Garnish with the spring onions and Chinese parsley, serve immediately.

Braised Xiao Bai Cai (top) and Braised Abalone and Sea Cucumber with Baby Kailan.

Sizzling chicken with shallots in clay pot

Serves 10

600 g	Whole chicken, deboned
1/2 tsp	Salt
500 mL	Vegetable oil
1 tsp	Flour

40 g	Black beans, steamed	
80 g	Green capsicum, cut into cubes	
40 g	Red capsicum, cut into cubes	} A
40 g	Ginger, finely minced	
20 g	Garlic	

80 g	Spring onions
20 g	Celery
240 mL	Clear chicken stock
30 g	Shallots, sliced
1 tbsp	Oyster sauce
1/2 tsp	Sugar
1 tsp	Sesame oil

PREPARATION AND PRESENTATION

Wash and debone the chicken, and cut into serving-sized pieces. Marinate for 5 minutes in 1/2 tsp of salt, 1 tsp of flour and 1/2 tsp of sesame oil.

Heat a wok, and pour in the 500 mL of oil. Add the chicken pieces and stir-fry for about 5 minutes over medium-high heat. Add the shallots and stir-fry for another minute. Remove chicken pieces and set aside. Drain excess oil.

Add ingredients A to the wok and toss for 30 seconds until fragrant. Return the chicken pieces and continue tossing.

Pour in the stock and simmer for 5 minutes.

Add the oyster sauce, sugar, and 1/2 teaspoon of sesame oil, then add the spring onions and celery. Allow to boil over medium heat.

When the sauce boils, pour it into a claypot. Put the lid on the pot and place on the stove, on high, for 2 - 3 minutes to heat the claypot.

Just before serving, heat some oil in a wok. Pour the heated oil around the rim of the claypot lid to create the sizzling effect. Serve immediately.

Stir-fried kailan topped with black mushrooms

Serves 10

440 g	Kailan
6	Black mushrooms

250 mL	Stock	
2	Ginger slices	} A
1 tbsp	Vegetable oil	

4 tbsp	Vegetable oil
3 tsp	Sugar
320 mL	Stock
1/2 tsp	Oyster sauce

PREPARATION AND PRESENTATION

Soak the mushrooms in water for 2 hours. Remove and cut off stems. Rinse in water to remove impurities.

In the cooking pot, add the mushrooms and ingredients A and allow to boil for 1 1/2 hours over medium heat.

Wash kailan in water. Add 4 tbsp of vegetable oil and 3 tsp of sugar to a pot of boiling water and blanch kailan for about 1 minute. Drain and place on a serving plate.

Heat a wok and add mushrooms, 320 mL of stock and 1/2 tsp oyster sauce. Stir-fry for about 1 minute. Add cornstarch for thickening, if necessary.

Remove black mushroom from wok and place over the kailan, top with remaining sauce. Serve immediately.

Stir-fried Asparagus with Scallops in Black Pepper (right) and Steamed Red Grouper with Black Bean Sauce.

STIR-FRIED ASPARAGUS WITH SCALLOPS IN BLACK PEPPER

Serves 10

400 g	Green asparagus, cut into 3-cm pieces
10	Fresh scallops (approx. 40 g per piece)
100 mL	Water
1 tsp	Salt
20 g	Garlic, minced
1 tbsp	Crushed black pepper

1 tsp	Oyster sauce	
150 mL	Supreme broth, see recipe on page 126	A
¹/₂ tsp	Sugar	
¹/₂ tsp	Sesame oil	

2 tbsp	Chinese rice wine
2 tbsp	Cornflour mixture (1 part flour to 4 parts water)

PREPARATION AND PRESENTATION

Blanch the scallops in boiling water for 3 minutes. Drain and set aside.

Heat a wok, add some oil and stir-fry the asparagus quickly. Drain and set aside.

Bring 100 mL of water to a boil, add the salt and the asparagus, and allow to boil for 2 - 3 minutes. Drain the asparagus and set aside.

Add more oil to the wok. Stir-fry the scallops for 1 minute over high heat, remove and set aside.

Using the same wok, stir-fry the garlic and black pepper, then add the asparagus and scallops.

Add ingredients A, stir-fry over high heat, mixing all the ingredients thoroughly, then pour in the Chinese rice wine. Mix well. Add the cornflour mixture to thicken if necessary. Remove from heat and serve immediately.

Chef's Notes
– This is Cantonese cooking at its best. The *al dente* asparagus is perfectly complemented by the slightly underdone scallops and fragrant sauce.

EGG NOODLES WITH CRABMEAT, STRAW MUSHROOMS AND CHOY SUM IN SOUP

Serves 10

1 kg	Whole fresh chicken
3 L	Water
500 g	Fresh Chinese egg noodles
2 tsp	Salt
¹/₂ tsp	Sesame oil
1 tbsp	Cooking oil
250 g	Straw mushrooms, cut in half
250 g	Fresh crabmeat, cleaned
4 tbsp	Cornflour mixture (1 part flour to 4 parts water)

Garnish

20 stalks	Baby choy sum, blanched
10	Crab claws, cooked

PREPARATION AND PRESENTATION

Boil the chicken for 4 hours. Remove the chicken and retain the stock.

Blanch the egg noodles in boiling water for 5 minutes then rinse in cold water. Place in a large serving bowl.

In a wok, heat 1 L of chicken stock, add the salt and sesame oil, then bring to a boil. Pour the mixture into the large bowl of noodles.

Place 200 mL of the chicken stock in the heated wok and add the straw mushrooms and crabmeat.

Quickly bring to a boil.

Thicken with the cornflour mixture if necessary.

Add the mixture to the noodles. Garnish with the blanched choy sum and cooked crab claws, serve at once with XO Chilli Sauce.

Chef's Notes
– XO Chilli Sauce is a spicy yet fragrant composition. To prepare 1 L of the sauce, do the following:

200 g	Chilli padi, stem removed
200 g	Garlic, whole
180 mL	Chilli oil
300 mL	Vegetable oil

150 g	Dried shrimps	
200 g	Yunnan ham	Finely blended
4	Dried scallops	

Pour 100 mL of vegetable oil into a blender, add whole garlic and blend. Remove mixture and set aside. Wash blender. Pour another 100 mL of oil in the blender and add chilli padi. Blend well. Remove and set aside. Heat the wok, add garlic mixture and stir-fry till fragrant. Then, add chilli padi mixture and continue to stir-fry for 1 minute over high heat. Add chilli oil and stir well. Lastly, add the finely blended Yunnan ham, dried shrimps and scallops. Mix well.

Egg Noodles with Crabmeat, Straw Mushrooms and Choy Sum in Soup. Following pages: A fine selection of Cantonese Dim Sum.

Stir-fried Milk with Crabmeat, Roe and Deep-fried Crab Claws

Serves 10

500 mL	Fresh milk
400 g	Egg white
200 g	Fresh crabmeat
100 g	Fresh crab roe
50 g	Cornflour
10 g	Chinese parsley
1 L	Vegetable oil
10	Crab claws
1/2 tsp	Salt
3 tbsp	Flour

PREPARATION AND PRESENTATION

1. Stir-fried milk with crabmeat and roe
   Add the fresh milk to the cornflour, then the egg white and salt. Mix well.
   Separate the mixture into two equal portions and set aside.
   In a stainless-steel bowl, immerse the crab roe in hot water for 5 seconds. Drain and set aside.
   Heat a wok and add 500 mL of the oil. When the oil is hot, turn off the heat and slowly add 1 portion of the milk mixture. Gently toss until the mixture has a custard-like consistency, then drain off the oil.
   Pour the remaining milk mixture into the wok and toss with a spatula over low heat until almost cooked. Add the fresh crabmeat and crab roe, and toss until cooked. Arrange on a serving dish.
2. Deep-fried crab claws
   Bring a pot of water to the boil, add the crab claws and a pinch of salt and allow to boil for 5 minutes, then drain. Remove the lower half of the shell from the claws.
   Heat 500 mL of oil in a wok. Coat the claw with a thin layer of flour and deep-fry.
   Remove the deep-fried claws from the wok and arrange around the stir-fried milk with crabmeat and roe. Sprinkle with Chinese parsley to garnish the dish and serve immediately with a light soya sauce.

Chef's Note
− This dish requires a deft hand with the wok as the milk mixture burns easily.

Sautéed Crystal Prawns

Serves 10

10	Fresh jumbo prawns, 140 g per piece
1 tsp	Lye water (see Chef's Note of caution below)
1 L	Water
20 g	Salt
15 g	Cornflour
1/2 tsp	Sesame oil
500 mL	Vegetable oil

Garnish
50 g	Young ginger, finely shredded
100 g	Spring onions, finely shredded

PREPARATION AND PRESENTATION

Shell and devein the prawns. Wash in fresh water.
Add the lye water to the fresh water and soak the prawns for 30 minutes. Drain and place the prawns in a deep pot. Rinse them under running water for about 1/2 hour to ensure that the residual lye water is completely washed away.
Pat dry with a towel and add salt, cornflour and sesame oil. Place the ginger and spring onions on a serving plate.
Heat a wok and add oil. Add the prawns and stir-fry continously for 30 seconds. Drain off the oil.
Add the salt, sugar and sesame oil, then continue stir-frying until the prawns are cooked. Arrange the prawns on the layer of ginger and spring onions and serve immediately.

Chef's Note
− Lye water is used by many Chinese chefs to give prawns a crisp-like texture when stir-frying. As it is an alkaline-based mixture, lye water should be used sparingly and with caution.

Double-Boiled Bird's Nest with Almonds.

CHINESE SWEET DUET

Special equipment: 15-cm square, 3-cm height baking tin

Serves 10

Glutinous Custard Dumplings

240 g	Glutinous rice flour
80 g	Lard
240 mL	Water
40 mL	Coconut milk, preferably fresh
40 g	Flour

40 g	Butter	
80 mL	Fresh milk	
80 g	Flour	
2	Eggs	} A
240 g	Custard sugar	
20 g	Milk powder	
20 g	Castor sugar	
40 g	Dessicated coconut	

1½ tsp	Strawberry jam

Deep-fried Lotus Paste Puffs

400 g	Flour
160 g	Lard
20 g	Sesame seeds
160 g	Lotus paste
2	Salted egg yolks
80 mL	Vegetable oil
240 mL	Water

PREPARATION AND PRESENTATION

1. Skin for glutinous custard dumplings

   Mix the glutinous rice flour and the water thoroughly in a large bowl. Add the lard and coconut juice to the flour and mix thoroughly. Pour the mixture into the mould and steam for 20 minutes. Remove and allow to cool.

2. Custard

   Combine ingredients A thoroughly in a mixer. Steam for 10 minutes.

   Remove from the heat and whisk again. Steam for another 15 minutes. Allow to cool.

3. Dumplings

   Turn the glutinous rice mixture onto a wooden board and roll into a 2.5-cm tube. Divide into 12 equal parts. On a wooden board, roll the glutinous rice flour into a 1-cm diameter tube.

   Flatten each part separately with your palm. Form the custard into 12 small balls with your hands.

   Wrap the glutinous rice flour around the custard ball, covering it completely. Roll the balls in a plate of dessicated coconut.

   Dot the top of each glutinous custard dumpling with strawberry jam.

4. Deep-fried lotus paste puffs

   Combine 130 g of the flour with the lard in a mixer. Remove and set aside.

   Mix the remaining flour with the water.

   Pour the flour and water mixture over the flour and lard. Form into a rectangular shape about 2-cm thick. Trim the sides.

   Roll the rectangle into the shape of a tube. Divide into 12 equal parts and flatten with your palm.

   Divide the lotus paste into 12 equal parts. Do the same with the salted-egg yolk.

   Place 1 part of the lotus paste and 1 part of the salted egg yolk in the centre of the flattened dough. Wrap the dough completely around the lotus paste and yolk.

   Heat a wok, add the oil and deep-fry the puffs over medium heat for 2 minutes.

   Raise the heat and deep-fry to a golden-brown. Serve with the glutinous custard dumplings.

CHILLED CREAM OF SAGO WITH MANGO

Serves 10

150 g	Sago pearls
2 L	Water
220 g	Sugar
110 mL	Water
1 L	Fresh milk
200 g	Sweetened full cream-condensed milk
300 g	Mango ice-cream
300 g	Coconut milk, preferably fresh
3	Mango, skinned, seeded and cut into ½-cm cubes

PREPARATION AND PRESENTATION

Soak sago pearls in 1 L of cold water and drain. Cook in 1 L of hot water for 10 minutes. Drain and rinse under running water for 5 minutes. Set aside.

Boil sugar in 110 mL of water till the sugar dissolves. Set aside.

Mix fresh milk, sweetened condensed milk and sugar syrup. Pour in the cooked sago pearls and stir well to prevent them from sticking together.

Add mango ice-cream, coconut milk and mango cubes.

DOUBLE-BOILED BIRD'S NEST WITH ALMONDS

Serves 10

200 g	Dried bird's nest, superior quality
Garnish	
200 g	Whole Chinese almonds
300 g	White rock sugar
2 slices	Young ginger
1.2 L	Water

PREPARATION AND PRESENTATION

Soak the bird's nest in water for 5 hours, then drain. Ensure that all impurities are removed from the bird's nest.

Place the rock sugar and ginger in a double boiler for 20 - 30 minutes, until the sugar has dissolved. Remove and set aside.

Pound the almonds until very fine. Transfer to a pot and boil in 500 mL of water. Strain the mixture when the water boils, and set aside.

Divide the rock sugar, almond mixture and bird's nest into 10 porcelain containers and seal tightly with plastic wrap. Double-boil for 4 hours. Serve hot.

Chef's Note
- Superior quality bird's nest is very high in protein, and its taste is similar to that of poultry eggs.

Chapter Six

DOC CHENG'S

*I*nnovative. Quirky. Unexpected. Welcome to the world of Doc Cheng's, where dining is never dull. Since its opening in 1995, the award-winning restaurant has cultivated a loyal following for its inventive East-meets-West cuisine and stylish ambience.

Here the emphasis is on light and nutritious dishes composed of the freshest ingredients and prepared with sensitivity. Food preparation is part of the dining experience as chefs toil under the Chinese pagoda-style roof of the central exhibition kitchen. Attention to detail extends to the friendly service as courses are served on fused glass plates in interesting shapes, textures and colours, while forks and knives can be turned upside-down and used as chopsticks. The cuisine can be described as trans-ethnic and is underscored by a traditional Asian philosophy: food as nourishment for the body, mind and spirit.

Inspiration for the popular restaurant came from the exploits of Doctor Cheng Soon Wen, MD, FRCS. The good doctor was a great believer in the restorative powers of food and drink, preferring to prescribe a stiff Scotch or a warm broth rather than a boxful of pills.

Legend has it that the Penang-born son of a wealthy rubber trading family became "a connoisseur of fine wines, good food and nubile women" at an early age when he moved to Singapore with his widowed mother. The well-travelled doctor studied medicine in London where he freely sampled the flavours of the world in the bohemian restaurants of the city: the Italian cafés of Soho, the French bistros of Chelsea, and the Spanish tapas bars in Brompton Road.

After several years of indulgence in Europe, Doc Cheng returned to Singapore and set up practice on Beach Road, just a few doors away from Raffles. The hotel's attractions proved irresistible and it wasn't long before he was dispensing his own peculiar brand of medicine from the hotel. Doc Cheng was for many years a lively feature of life at Raffles right up to the war. *Bon vivant* and raconteur, he could often take a couple of hours for a consultation during which he would dispense good advice, good humour and hearty friendship to any "patient" within earshot.

Today Doc Cheng's signature Restorative Tonic graces the tables not only of Raffles Hotel, but of Raffles International's hotels in Bangkok, Hamburg, Geneva and Amsterdam.

Doc Cheng's, a trendsetting dining concept that marries the best of the East and West.

APPETIZERS

Blackened Ahi and Duck Liver Crisp with Avocado and Pickled Mango

Serves 4

Blackened Ahi

200 g	Sashimi-grade Ahi (Hawaiian yellowfin tuna), cut into 4-by-2-by-6-cm blocks

Blackening Spice

1 tsp	Chilli powder
1 tsp	Paprika
1 tsp	Cayenne pepper
1 tsp	Shichimi togarashi
1 tsp	Sea salt
1 tsp	Freshly ground black pepper

Duck Liver Crisp

100 g	Duck liver
	Sea salt
	Freshly ground black pepper

Avocado

1	Avocado, peeled
¹/₂	Red onion, finely diced
10 g	Chinese parsley, chopped
3 tbsp	Vine-ripened tomatoes, finely chopped
1 tsp	Lemon juice
10 g	Pickled ginger
1 tsp	Sesame oil
	Sea salt
	Freshly ground black pepper

Pickled Mango

80 g	Pickled mango, diced
¹/₂	Onion, finely diced
25 g	Red bell peppers, roasted and finely diced
10 g	Chinese parsley, chopped
1 tbsp	Lime juice
15 g	Jalapenos, finely diced
	Sea salt
	Freshly ground black pepper

Garnish

1 tbsp	Srirachi
8 sheets	Wonton skin, deep-fried
4 sprigs	Chervil
4 sprigs	Shiso buds

PREPARATION AND PRESENTATION

1. Blackened Ahi
   Combine the blackening spice ingredients in a bowl and mix well.
   Coat the tuna with the spice mix on one side.
   Using a very hot cast-iron skillet, sear the tuna quickly on all sides. It should remain uncooked in the centre.
   Set aside to cool, then cut it into 16 even slices, allocating 4 slices to each portion.

2. Duck liver crisp
   Season the duck liver with salt and pepper, and pan-fry until it is medium rare.
   Set aside to cool, then cut into 8 even slices, allocating 2 slices to each portion.

3. Avocado
   Place the avocado in a bowl and mash it gently with a fork. The mash should be slightly chunky.
   Add the remaining ingredients and toss lightly.
   Season to taste.

4. Pickled mango
   Combine all the ingredients in a bowl and mix well.
   Season to taste.

5. To finish and serve
   Drizzle the srirachi on 4 plates and spoon a dollop of avocado on each plate.
   Top this with a wonton crisp, then top the wonton crisp with a dollop of avocado.
   Place 2 slices of tuna and a slice of duck liver on the avocado and spoon some pickled mango over.
   Repeat this layering process again.
   Garnish each portion with a sprig of chervil and a sprig of shiso buds to serve.

Chef's Notes

– Use quality sashimi-grade tuna. Fresh tuna should be firm yet soft to the touch and deep red in colour.
– Leave the avocado pit in the mash and it will retain its colour for a longer time.
– Adjust the proportion of ingredients for the blackening spice as desired.
– Srirachi is a smooth Asian chilli paste and is available in gourmet supermarkets.
– Vegetarians may use an assortment of mushrooms to replace the tuna and duck liver.

Blackened Ahi and Duck Liver Crisp with Avocado and Pickled Mango.

WOK-SEARED BLACK PEPPER BEEF AND ASPARAGUS SALAD WITH CHARRED SARAWAK PINEAPPLE AND PISTACHIO VINAIGRETTE

Serves 4

Wok-Seared Black Pepper Beef

8	Beef tenderloin fillets (30 g each)
3 tbsp	Oyster sauce
2 tbsp	Garlic, minced
2 tbsp	Ginger, minced
1 tsp	Freshly ground black pepper
30 mL	Peanut oil
20 mL	Chinese cooking wine

Salad

12	Baby green asparagus, wok-seared
12	Shiitake mushrooms, wok-seared
60 g	Frisée
50 g	Watercress
40 g	Endive, julienned
	Sea salt
	Freshly ground black pepper

Vinaigrette

120 g	Pineapple, finely diced
1 tbsp	Shallots, minced
1 tbsp	Ginger, minced
120 mL	Pineapple juice
20 g	Chinese parsley stems
1	Chilli padi with seeds, minced
20 g	Chinese parsley leaves
30 mL	Olive oil
30 mL	Grapeseed oil
60 mL	Rice vinegar
	Sea salt
	Freshly ground black pepper

Garnish

2 tbsp	Pistachios, crushed and roasted
1/2 tsp	White sesame seeds, toasted
1/2 tsp	Black sesame seeds, toasted
10 g	Wonton noodles, deep-fried
40 g	Goat's cheese, cut into bite-sized pieces and dusted with toasted white and black sesame seeds

PREPARATION AND PRESENTATION

1. Wok-seared black pepper beef
   Marinate the beef in all the ingredients, except the peanut oil and Chinese cooking wine, for 2 hours. Heat the peanut oil in a wok and when it is smoking, add the beef fillets one at a time.
   Sear the beef, in two batches, for 5 – 10 seconds on each side (medium rare). When it is almost ready, deglaze with the Chinese cooking wine.
2. Salad
   Combine all the ingredients in a bowl and toss lightly. Season to taste.
3. Vinaigrette
   In a hot wok, cook the pineapple until golden brown. Add the shallots, ginger, pineapple juice, Chinese parsley stems and chilli padi, and reduce by half. Remove the Chinese parsley stems and add the remaining ingredients. Mix well.
4. To finish and serve
   Divide the salad among 4 plates and top each portion with a slice of wok-seared black pepper beef.
   Drizzle the vinaigrette over and around. Sprinkle the pistachios and sesame seeds over, and garnish with some deep-fried noodles and goat's cheese to serve.

Chef's Note
- Charring the pineapple in a wok over high heat gives it added flavour.
- The wok must be very hot for the beef to caramelise nicely.

Wok-Seared Black Pepper Beef and Asparagus Salad with Charred Sarawak Pineapple and Pistachio Vinaigrette..

MAIN COURSES

PAN-ROASTED TASMANIAN BARRAMUNDI AND FORBIDDEN RICE WITH LOBSTER AND CURRY NAGE

Special equipement: Electric hand-held blender

Serves 4

Barramundi

4	Barramundi fillets (120 g each)
2 tbsp	Olive oil
	Sea salt
	Freshly ground black pepper

Vegetables

80 g	Baby bok choy
2 tbsp	Peanut oil
2 tbsp	Oyster sauce

Forbidden Rice

500 g	Thai black rice
450 mL	Chicken stock (see recipe, page 40)
25 g	Ginger root
2 cloves	Garlic
2 cloves	Shallots
	Sea salt
	Freshly ground black pepper

Lobster Nage

6	Lobster heads, crushed
300 g	Leeks, chopped
300 g	Onions, chopped
300 g	Carrots, chopped
300 g	Celery, chopped
1	Bay leaf
20 g	Basil
20 g	Thyme
4	Vine-ripened tomatoes
3 tbsp	Tomato paste
250 mL	Brandy
2 L	Heavy cream
	Sea salt
	Freshly ground black pepper

Curry Nage

2 tbsp	Seasme oil
25 g	Garlic
25 g	Ginger
80 g	Onion
25 g	Kaffir lime leaves, minced
40 g	Lemon grass, minced
3	Chilli padi, minced
25 g	Chinese parsley
30 mL	Palm sugar
30 mL	Tomato paste
90 mL	Red curry paste
2 L	Coconut milk
	Sea salt
	Freshly ground black pepper

Garnish

120 g	Macadamia nuts, roasted
2 tsp	Chives, chopped
5 g	Spring onion, cut into strips and soaked in iced water for 5 minutes
1 tsp	Benitate (Japanese pepper cress)

PREPARATION AND PRESENTATION

1. Barramundi
   Season the fish with salt and pepper.
   Heat the olive oil in a skillet and pan-roast the fish for about 2 minutes on each side (medium).

2. Vegetables
   Blanch the baby bok choy in salted boiling water.
   Heat the peanut oil in a wok and quickly sauté the vegetables in the oyster sauce for 10 seconds.

3. Forbidden rice
   Soak the Thai black rice in cold water for 30 minutes. Strain and combine the rice and all the remaining ingredients in a pot. Bring to a boil, then reduce the heat to medium. Cover the pot and simmer for 20 minutes. Discard the ginger, garlic and shallots.

4. Lobster nage
   In a pan, roast the lobster heads with the leeks, onions, carrots and celery in a preheated 180°C oven until the heads are bright red.
   Add the remaining ingredients, except the brandy, heavy cream, salt and pepper, and roast for 5 minutes.
   Deglaze with the brandy, then add the heavy cream and return the pan to the oven. Reduce the mixture by half. Remove from the heat and allow the mixture to infuse for 30 minutes.
   Pass the mixture though a fine sieve. Using the hand-held blender, process the mixture until well incorporated. Season to taste.

5. Curry nage
   In heavy-bottom pot, heat the oil and sauté all the ingredients, except the palm sugar, tomato paste, coconut milk and red curry paste, until fragrant.
   Add the palm sugar, tomato paste and red curry paste, and mix well. Add the coconut milk and reduce by half.
   Pass the mixture through a fine sieve. Season to taste.

6. To finish and serve
   Place a ring mould in the centre of a plate and fill it with the forbidden rice.
   Pat the rice down firmly and top it with the vegetables.
   Top the vegetables with a serving of barramundi.
   Spoon the lobster nage and curry nage around.
   Sprinkle the macadamia nuts around, and garnish with the chopped chives, spring onion and benitate to serve.

Chef's Note

– Use any white fish of your choice. Good substitutes for barramundi are mahi mahi, sea bass and snapper.
– You may also grill the fish instead of pan-roasting it.

Pan-Roasted Tasmanian Barramundi and Forbidden Rice with Lobster and Curry Nage

SOUTHEAST ASIAN-STYLE STEAMED MAHI MAHI WITH GRILLED CHANTERELLE SALAD AND CARROT-CITRUS BROTH

Serves 4

Steamed Mahi Mahi

4	Mahi mahi fillets (120 g each)

Thai Seasoning

30 g	Lemon grass, minced
10 g	Kaffir lime leaves, minced
20 mL	Sesame oil
10 mL	Grapeseed oil
15 g	Chinese parsley, chopped
1	Chilli padi, minced

Grilled Chanterelle Salad

200 g	Chanterelle mushrooms
2 tbsp	Olive oil
100 g	Kang kong (water spinach)
80 g	Onions, sliced
80 g	Red bell peppers, julienned
15 g	Shallots, sliced
80 g	Watercress
	Sea salt
	Freshly ground black pepper

Carrot-Citrus Broth

60 mL	Fish sauce
30 mL	Sambal paste
120 mL	Lime juice
60 mL	Water
30 mL	Olive oil
60 mL	Sugar
30 mL	Lemon juice
30 mL	Rice vinegar
30 mL	Peanuts, roasted and crushed
80 mL	Fresh carrot juice
15 g	Chinese parsley, chopped

Garnish

10 g	Green papaya, julienned
10 g	Pomelo sacs
1 tbsp	Red chilli, julienned
10 g	Mango, julienned
10 g	Chinese parsley, roughly chopped

PREPARATION AND PRESENTATION

1. Steamed mahi mahi
   Marinate the mahi mahi in the Thai seasoning ingredients for 1 hour.
   Line a steamer with a bamboo leaf and place the fish on top. The bamboo leaf gives the fish more flavour.
   Steam for 6 - 7 minutes until the fish is cooked evenly.

2. Grilled chanterelle salad
   Toss the chanterelles in the olive oil and season to taste. Grill them to desired doneness.
   In a separate pan, sauté the red bell peppers, onions and kang kong in olive oil and season to taste.
   Combine all the vegetables in a bowl and toss well.

3. Carrot-citrus broth
   Combine all the ingredients in a bowl and whisk until the sugar dissolves.
   Let it stand for 6 hours for the flavours to infuse.

4. To finish and serve
   Divide the grilled chanterelle salad among 4 plates and top each portion with a serving of steamed mahi mahi.
   Garnish with the green papaya, pomelo sacs, red chilli, mango and Chinese parsley.
   Ladle the carrot-citrus broth around to serve.

Chef's Notes
- Carrot juice gives this dish its attractive colour and natural sweetness.
- Any kind of seafood, especially lobsters and prawns, may be used to prepare this dish.
- The carrot-citrus broth may also be used as a salad dressing.
- Vegetarians may replace the fish with rice.

Southeast Asian-style Steamed Mahi Mahi with Grilled Chanterelle Salad and Carrot-Citrus Broth.

GRILLED SZECHUAN RACK OF LAMB WITH BRAISED KAILAN AND PORT WINE GINGER DEMI

Special equipement: Electric hand-held blender

Serves 4

Vegetable Stock

30 mL	Vegetable oil
30 g	Carrots, medium-diced
60 g	Onions, medium-diced
60 g	Leeks, medium-diced
30 g	Celery, medium-diced
30 g	Green cabbage, chopped
30 g	Turnips, chopped
30 g	Tomatoes, chopped
2 cloves	Garlic, unpeeled
2.1 L	Water
1 sprig	Parsley
1	Bay leaf
1 sprig	Thyme
10	Black peppercorns
2	Cloves
1 tsp	Fennel seeds
	Salt

Szechuan Rack of Lamb

600 g	Rack of lamb, cleaned and trimmed
60 mL	Light soya sauce
10 g	Garlic
10 g	Ginger

Coating

150 mL	Hoisin sauce
50 mL	Sambal paste
2 tbsp	Szechuan peppercorns, toasted

Port Wine Ginger Demi

20 g	Star anise
20 g	Tarragon
80 g	Ginger
250 mL	Port wine
150 mL	Red wine
500 mL	Veal stock (see recipe, pages 58 and 60)
	Sea salt
	Freshly ground black pepper

Sweet Potato Mash

250 g	Sweet potato, peeled
1	Ginger root, peeled
5 cloves	Garlic, peeled
2 tbsp	Butter
3 tbsp	Honey
	Sea salt
	Freshly ground black pepper

Pandan Cream

25 g	Ginger
25 g	Garlic
25 g	Shallots
200 mL	Dry white wine
200 mL	Heavy cream
25 g	Pandan leaves
100 g	Coconut milk

Braised Kailan

1 tsp	Peanut oil
2 tsp	Oyster sauce
500 mL	Vegetable stock
120 g	Kailan
75 g	Baby carrots
75 g	Lotus roots, cut into pieces

Curry Oil

250 g	Curry powder
250 mL	Corn oil

Garnish

4	Sweet potato chips
4 bouquets	Thyme, rosemary, tarragon and Italian parsley

PREPARATION AND PRESENTATION

1. Vegetable stock
   In a stockpot, heat the oil and sauté the vegetables for 3 - 5 minutes. Add the water, herbs and spices, and bring to a simmer for 30 - 40 minutes, skimming from time to time. Season to taste and pass the mixture through a fine sieve.

2. Szechuan rack of lamb
   Marinate the lamb in the remaining ingredients overnight. Combine the coating ingredients in a bowl. Mix well. Sear the lamb over an open grill and brush on the coating. Place in a preheated 180°C oven for 8 - 10 minutes (medium). Rest the lamb for 3 - 4 minutes before slicing.

3. Port wine ginger demi
   Reduce the veal stock to sauce consistency. Place all the ingredients, except the stock, in a pot and bring to a boil. Reduce the mixture by half, add the stock and cook for 15 minutes over medium heat. Season to taste and pass the mixture through a fine sieve.

4. Sweet potato mash
   Place all the ingredients, except the butter, honey, salt and pepper, in a pot. Cook until they are soft. Strain, discard the ginger and garlic, and pass the sweet potato through a ricer. Whip the mash with the honey and butter. Season to taste.

5. Pandan cream
   Place all the ingredients in a pot and bring to a boil. Reduce for 15 minutes to a sauce consistency. Pass the mixture through a fine sieve. Process it with a hand-held blender until well incorporated.

6. Braised kailan
   Combine the oil, oyster sauce and vegetable stock in a pot and bring to a boil. Add the carrots and lotus roots. Braise until just cooked. Add the kailan and braise for 1 minute.

7. Curry oil
   Combine the curry powder and corn oil in a pot. Simmer for 10 minutes. Pass the mixture through a fine sieve.

8. To finish and serve
   Place the sweet potato mash on 4 plates and arrange the vegetables, sweet potato chips and lamb on the side. Spoon the port ginger demi and pandan cream around. Drizzle the curry oil over. Garnish with the herb bouquets to serve.

Grilled Szechuan Rack of Lamb with Braised Kailan and Port Wine Ginger Demi.

DESSERT

Warm Sesame-Chocolate Cake with Haupia Ice Cream and Mango Sauce

Special equipment: 10 aluminium soufflé tins with base 4-cm of diameter and 5-cm depth

Serves 10

Warm Sesame-Chocolate Cake

90 g	Bitter sweet chocolate
15 g	Tahini (sesame paste)
90 g	Butter
2	Eggs
2	Egg yolks
80 g	Sugar
30 g	Plain flour, sifted

Haupia Ice Cream

250 mL	Heavy cream
250 mL	Coconut milk
1 tbsp	Grated coconut flesh
4	Egg yolks
200 g	Sugar
1 tsp	Malibu liqueur

Mango Sauce

500 g	Fresh mango, chopped
250 mL	Fresh mango juice
2 tbsp	Fresh lime juice
500 mL	Water
500 g	Sugar
1	Vanilla pod

Brochette of Fresh Fruit

5 g	Watermelon, cut into 2-cm cubes
5 g	Dragonfruit, cut into 2-cm cubes
5 g	Rock melon, cut into 2-cm cubes
5 g	Mango, cut into 2-cm cubes
4	Lemon grass skewers

Chocolate Chip Tuile

12 g	Flour
62 g	Sugar
31 g	Chocolate chips
12 mL	Fresh orange juice
31 g	Butter, melted
10 g	Pistachios, chopped

Coconut Chips

5 g	Fresh coconut flesh, cut into strips

Garnish

1 tsp	Icing sugar
8	Sansho leaves

PREPARATION AND PRESENTATION

1. Warm sesame-chocolate cake
   Preheat the oven to 180°C. Melt the bitter chocolate, tahini and butter in a double boiler.
   Place the eggs, egg yolks and sugar in a bowl and whisk on high speed until the mixture is light and fluffy (about three times its original volume).
   Add the melted chocolate mixture and whisk slowly to mix. Gently fold in the flour.
   Butter the soufflé tins evenly, then fill them with the chocolate mixture. Level and bake in the oven for approximately 9 – 10 minutes. To check whether the cake is ready, insert a skewer or the point of a very fine knife into the centre; it should come out clean.
   Remove from the oven and unmould onto plates.

2. Haupia ice cream
   Combine all the ingredients an ice cream machine and process as instructed.
   Keep refrigerated until required or for up to 1 week if using fresh coconut milk.

3. Mango sauce
   Scrape the beans from the vanilla pod and combine them with the remaining ingredients in a pan and bring to a boil. Set aside to cool.
   Process in a blender until smooth.

4. Brochette of fresh fruit
   Gently skewer the fruit with the lemon grass sticks.

5. Chocolate chip tuile
   Preheat the oven to 180°C. Combine all the dry ingredients in a bowl and mix well.
   Add the orange juice and melted butter and mix well. Spread the batter thinly on a baking sheet and sprinkle the chopped pistachios over. Bake in the oven for 5 minutes until crispy and golden brown.
   Set aside to cool. Break into smaller pieces to serve.

6. Coconut chips
   Preheat the oven to 150°C. Bake the coconut strips in the oven for 10 minutes until crispy.

7. To finish and serve
   Lightly dust the cakes with icing sugar.
   Spoon the mango sauce and the haupia ice cream across the plates as shown.
   Top each cake with a scoop of ice cream and garnish with a brochette of fresh fruit, a coconut chip, 2 chocolate chip tuiles and sansho leaves to serve.

Chef's Notes

- Haupia is a traditional Hawaiian coconut custard dessert. In this recipe, we have prepared an ice cream using the same ingredients.
- If tahini (sesame paste) is unavailable, use peanut butter.
- Cupcake tins may be used in place of ring moulds.
- If sansho leaves are unavailable, substitute with any other edible flowers or leaves.

Warm Sesame-Chocolate Cake with Haupia Ice Cream and Mango Sauce.

GLOSSARY

BASMATI RICE

A fragrant, long-grained rice originating from Pakistan. Basmati rice is used in many Indian rice dishes and has a marvellous nutty flavour.

BEANCURD

Generally bland in flavour, beancurd is very nutritious and is delicious when prepared with spicy sauces. Referred to as tofu or tahu in the recipes, it is also locally known as tauhu.

BIRD'S NEST

Highly prized by the Chinese and rather expensive, it is generally flavourless but is well known for its medicinal value. Bird's nest is gelatinous material used by swifts to line their nests. It should be cleaned of impurities and soaked in warm water before use.

BOMBAY (RED) ONIONS

Most Indian dishes require Bombay onions and it is important that these onions be used instead of other varieties. Substitute with Spanish onions if necessary.

BRIYANI SPICE

An Indian spice consisting of cinnamon, cloves, cardamom and black cumin.

CANDLENUTS
(BUAH KERAS)

Used in many local dishes, candlenuts are cream-coloured nuts similar to macadamias, which you may use as a substitute. Normally, they are finely ground before use.

CARDAMOM SEEDS
(BUAH PELAGA)

Small black seeds with an enticing lemon fragrance. Slightly bruise the seeds before use.

CHILLIES

Chillies are an integral part of Asian cooking and should not be confused with other members of the capsicum family. Chillies, rather than spices, are the source of heat for the curries and many of the other dishes in this book. Remember, though, that dishes need not be searingly hot to be authentic; in fact too many chillies tend to mask the flavours of a dish.

There are two main sizes of chillies. The more common is the long (10 - 15-cm) chilli, while the other variety is the small chilli padi (1-cm), which is fiery hot. Chillies are used in their unripe, green state or when they are ripe and red. The seeds are the hottest part, so remove them to retain the flavour but reduce the heat.

CHILLI PASTE

Dried red chillies, which lack the strong smell of fresh chillies, are used to make the chilli paste specified in many of the recipes in this book. Before grinding the chillies into a paste, whether with a mortar and pestle or an electric blender, tear each chilli into three or four pieces and soak them in hot water for about ten minutes. Squeeze out the excess moisture before grinding. You may find it convenient to buy a large amount of dried chillies and grind them into a coarse paste in a blender or food processor. The paste can then be stored in the freezer for future use. Be sure to thaw it before use.

CHILLI POWDER

A powdery seasoning made from ground dried red chillies. Not to be confused with the chilli powder available in the US, which contains a mixture of other spices and is much milder than the Singaporean variety.

CINNAMON
(KAYU MANIS)

The cinnamon mentioned in this book is sourced from the thick bark of the cassia tree. It is readily available in Singapore and most parts of the world.
Most of the recipes require only about 3 - 5-cm of cinnamon stick, unless otherwise indicated.

CLOVES

Frequently used in many local dishes, cloves are always used whole unless otherwise specified.

COCONUT

Fresh coconut milk is used for many of the recipes in this book. The rich milky juice is, in fact, an essential ingredient for many Asian dishes. A piece of muslin cloth can be used to extract the coconut milk from freshly grated coconut. Thick coconut milk comes from the first squeezing of grated coconut with a little water; thinner coconut milk comes from a second squeezing with considerably more water. The coconut milk referred to in this book usually comes from the first squeezing of the grated coconut.
To obtain thick coconut milk, place 500 g of freshly grated coconut in a muslin cloth, add $1/2$ cup of water and squeeze firmly.
To obtain thinner coconut milk, add $2^1/2$ cups of water to the once-squeezed, grated coconut and knead firmly.
The canned coconut milk found in many supermarkets and grocery stores around the world can be used in place of freshly grated coconut milk. If coconut cream has to be used, dilute with water to a lighter consistency.

CORIANDER SEEDS
(KETUMBAR)

A small round seed with a hint of orange fragrance, coriander is a frequently used curry spice.

CORIANDER LEAVES
(DAUN KETUMBAR, CHINESE PARSLEY)

Used for flavouring and garnishing many local dishes, the leaf has a faint peppery taste. It is also known as cilantro.

CURRY LEAVES
(DAUN KARI)

Small, dark-green leaves with a unique flavour, often used in southern Indian cuisine. Difficult to obtain in non-tropical climates.

CURRY POWDERS

A blend of spices that give curry dishes their distinctive flavour.
There are many recipes in this book that require the use of curry powder, in some instances, fish curry powder is needed, whereas in others, meat curry powder is necessary. No local cook worth his or her salt would ever consider substituting one for the other. Ready-mixed curry powder is generally available, and we suggest you purchase the best quality.
Do be aware that curry powders vary in composition, degree of hotness and freshness. When trying a new blend, some experimentation may be necessary until the desired flavour and intensity are obtained.
If not used frequently, curry powder will remain fresh almost indefinitely when stored in an air-tight container and placed in deep-freeze.

DHAL
(LENTILS)

Used extensively in Indian cooking, especially in vegetarian dishes. There are many varieties; those more commonly used are red, green and brown lentils.

DRIED SHRIMP PASTE
(BELACAN)

This paste is made from fermented shrimps and is readily available in Singapore. Dried shrimp paste has a very pungent smell before being cooked but adds a remarkable flavour to the dishes that require it.
For the sake of your family and friends, belacan should be stored in a tightly covered jar or the smell may pervade the house. Belacan can be kept indefinitely.
When a recipe calls for belacan, it is best to first flatten a piece to about 5-cm thickness and fry it in a dry pan for 2 - 3 minutes on each side. This particular method causes pungent smoke to be released, so make sure that your kitchen is well ventilated. Alternatively, you can grill the belacan in aluminium foil.

**FENNEL SEEDS
(JINTAN MANIS)**

Similar to cumin, fennel seeds have a sweet fragrance and flavour.

**FENUGREEK
(ALBA)**

A small seed with a bitter flavour, highly regarded for its medicinal properties. Fenugreek is often used in Indian recipes.

**FERMENTED SOYA BEANS
(TAU CHEO)**

Dark-brown beans used as a seasoning in many Singaporean dishes. Usually found in semi-paste form. Lightly pound to form a smooth paste before using.

FIVE-SPICE POWDER

Made from ground star anise, fennel, cloves, cinnamon and pepper, this powder will lose its flavour if kept too long.

**FRAGRANT LIME LEAF
(DAUN LIMAU PERUT)**

A sweet-smelling leaf also known as kaffir lime.

**GALANGAL
(BLUE GINGER, LENGKUAS)**

A member of the ginger family, galangal is also known as blue ginger and is frequently used in Malay cooking and has a delicate flavour.

GHEE

Clarified butter fat frequently used in Indian recipes. Unlike butter, ghee leaves no residue and does not burn during cooking.

**LEMON GRASS
(SERAI)**

A lemon-scented grass that is very important in Malay cooking. Use only the bottom 5 - 8-cm of the plant.

PANDAN LEAF

Also called fragrant screwpine, the pandan leaf is tied into a knot before use. For pandan juice, you will need 15 dark-green leaves to produce 2 tbsp. Shred the leaves finely, blend with 1 tbsp of water, and squeeze through a cheese cloth.

RICE WINE

Rice wine is found in most Chinese specialty stores. It can be replaced with dry sherry if necessary.

**SALTED BLACK BEANS
(TAU SEE)**

These small black beans are used in many Cantonese recipes and may be purchased from Chinese specialty stores. Usually sold moist in tins or jars, or dried in packets.

SHALLOTS

Many of the dishes in this book use fried shallots for garnish. To prepare, thinly slice the shallots and set aside. Heat vegetable oil for deep-frying until it is smoking, then add the shallots. Stir-fry over high heat until light brown. Reduce the heat and keep stirring until the shallots are golden brown. Remove, drain on absorbent paper and allow to cool. Fried shallots can be kept in an air-tight bottle for up to several months.

**STAR ANISE
(BUNGA LAWANG)**

Primarily used in Malay and Chinese cooking, this is a small, brown, star-shaped spice, and an ingredient in Chinese five-spice powder.

TAMARIND

To make juice from tamarind pulp, soak 1 tbsp of pulp in $^1/_4$ cup of warm water for 5 minutes. Squeeze the pulp with your fingers to extract the juice. Remove the seeds and fibrous matter.

If tamarind is unavailable, lemon or lime juice can be used as a substitute. However, the dish will not taste the same.

**TURMERIC
(KUNYIT)**

Fresh turmeric is usually chosen for its slightly bitter flavour. Some dishes, especially curries, require dry or powdered turmeric.

WEIGHTS AND MEASURES/ CONVERSION TABLES

Weights and measures used in this book are metric. A reliable set of gram/kilogram scales is recommended.

North American readers should note that the US (Imperial) to metric quantities listed are approximate conversions only. You may want to follow American Standard measurements and a gram/kilogram scale; to measure liquid or dry cup quantities you will also need a cup graduated in millilitres (mL) and litres (L).

WEIGHTS

Imperial	Metric
$^1/_2$ oz	15 g
1 oz	30 g
2 oz	60 g
3 oz	90 g
4 oz ($^1/_4$ lb)	125 g
6 oz	185 g
8 oz ($^1/_2$ lb)	250 g
12 oz ($^3/_4$ lb)	375 g
16 oz (1 lb)	500 g (0.5 kg)
24 oz (1$^1/_2$ lb)	750 g
32 g (2 lb)	1000 g (1 kg)
3 lb	1500 g (1.5 kg)
4 lb	2000 g (2 kg)

MEASURES

Imperial	Liquid Measures		Metric
1 fl oz			30 mL
2 fl oz	$^1/_4$	cup	
3 fl oz			100 mL
4 fl oz ($^1/_4$ US pint)	$^1/_2$	cup	125 mL
5 fl oz			150 mL
6 fl oz	$^3/_4$	cup	185 mL
8 fl oz ($^1/_2$ US pint)	1	cup	250 mL
10 fl oz	1$^1/_4$	cups	
12 fl oz	1$^1/_2$	cups	
14 fl oz	1$^3/_4$	cups	
16 fl oz	2	cups	500 mL
20 fl oz	2$^1/_2$	cups	

METRIC EQUIVALENTS

1 metric teaspoon	5 mL	
1 metric tablespoon	15 mL	
$^1/_4$ metric cup	60 mL	
$^1/_2$ metric cup	125 mL	
1 metric cup	250 mL ($^1/_4$ L)	
2 metric cups	500 mL ($^1/_2$ L)	
4 metric cups	1000 mL (1 L)	

TEMPERATURE

Fahrenheit	Gas Regulo	Celsius
225	1	105
250	2	120
275	3	135
300	4	150
325	5	165
350	6	175
375	7	190
400	8	205
425	9	220
450	10	230

(Note: Always pre-heat your oven 15 minutes before use.)